Hoofbeats, Hair Balls, and Three-Dog Nights:

Thirty Years of Pet Adventures

Lowell D. Streiker
Cartoons by Ron Rush

Alpine
PUBLICATIONS
Loveland, Colorado

Hoofbeats, Hair Balls and Three-Dog Nights: Thirty Years of Pet Adventures
Copyright © 2003 by Lowell D. Streiker
Cartoons © 2003 by Ron Rush

Library of Congress Cataloging-in-Publication Data

Streiker, Lowell D.
    Hoofbeats, hair balls, and three-dog nights: thirty years of pet adventures / Lowell D. Streiker ; cartoons by Ron Rush.
        p. cm.
    ISBN 1-57779-066-9
        1. Dogs--California--Cottonwood--Anecdotes. 2.
    Cats--California--Cottonwood--Anecdotes. 3.
    Horses--California--Cottonwood--Anecdotes. 4. Streiker, Lowell D. I. Title.

    SF426.2.S783 2004
    636.088'7--dc22   2004054556

The information contained in this book is complete and accurate to the best of our knowledge. All recommendations are made without guarantee on the part of the author or Alpine Publications, Inc. The author and publisher disclaim any liability with the use of this information.

This book is available at special quantity discounts for breeders and for club promotions, premiums, or educational use. Write for details.

For the sake of simplicity, the terms "he" or "she" are sometimes used to identify an animal or person. These are used in the generic sense only. No discrimination of any kind is intended toward either sex.

Many manufacturers secure trademark rights for their products. When Alpine Publications is aware of a trademark claim, we identify the product name by using initial capital letters.

Cover Design: Laura Newport
Editing: Betty J. McKinney, Deborah Helmers
Layout: Laura Newport
Cartoons: Ron Rush

First printing 2004

1 2 3 4 5 6 7 8 9 0

Printed in the United States of America.

Contents

With thanks to

Rita, Sherry, Peg, and Joan

Rescuers and Nurturers

Foreword

I was having a typically stressful day, trying to cram too much activity into too few hours. My overworked brain struggled to keep a sense of balance in the midst of the barrage of worries I fed it: "I ought to be doing . . . ," or "How am I going to get it all done?" or "Why didn't I . . . ?" My heart raced, my head ached; my joints hurt.

Reaching for the coffee pot (a quick fix for my anxiety), I fell over Bear, one of my eight dogs, snoring peacefully on his bed in the kitchen. In an awkward catch of myself on the way to the floor, I ended up beside him, my right hand landing easily on his soft head. He merely looked up at me as if to say, "Well, hello there; won't you join me?" And he was once again sleeping, completely unconcerned about anything at all.

I let my hand rest on him awhile, feeling the rise and fall of his body, his breath rhythmic, subtle, and centered. The only other sounds were the birds outside at the feeder and the deep purring of Noelle the cat as she slept in a nearby chair. Coffee forgotten, I allowed my eyes to settle into heaviness and close; heart rate slowed, blood pressure dropped, worries melted into gratefulness, and I snuggled down next to Bear and dozed. When, some minutes later, Bear stirred and stretched, I awoke feeling refreshed and ready for whatever activity remained in my day. My headache was gone, the stiffness eased, and a sense of the joy of things stood strong in my mind.

What amazing therapists these creatures are! The many who live under my care, or, more accurately look after me, remind me of what is truly important in life—this moment, where all the treasures are, the perfect balance of mind, body, and soul. It is a well-known, well-documented fact that being around an animal or two (or more, as in my case) lowers blood pressure, relieves depression, lessens anxiety, and brings much needed companionship (especially to the elderly and homebound). And animals make us laugh, one of the best therapies of all. Just watch ducks on a rainy day and you will find exuberant birds rushing hysterically happy from puddle to puddle. Or watch a cat playing with a leaf, or a dog defending the world from a frog . . . .

The animals that live with us care deeply about us—often, I believe, more than we do about them, only because they love us so unconditionally. They teach us to be complete, through their living, and their dying, through our memory of them, and that shared love we then carry over to others in our care. Without question, animals bless us greatly.

From his own experiences with the animals in his life, Lowell Streiker brings all of this into shining view in the book you now hold in your hands. He and his wife Connie without exception understand and honor what a gift the animal kingdom is to humankind. All the admirable qualities rest here in these pages—truth, joy, love, loyalty, humility, and peace. And in the total companionship—as the author so clearly demonstrates—between human and horse or dog or cat lies some of the best of healing on all levels.

—Rita M. Reynolds

Rita Reynolds is the founder of the Animals' Peace Garden, an animal sanctuary located in the foothills of the Blue Ridge Mountains near Charlottesville, Virginia. She tends to, and is lovingly taught by, her family of many elderly dogs, cats, donkeys, goats, ducks, chickens, and one cow. For the past twenty-five years her sanctuary has been home to hundreds of animals. Her primary work has focused on caring for elder animals and hospice care/conscious dying work with animals. Reynolds is the author of *Blessing the Bridge: What Animals Have to Teach Us About Death, Dying, and Beyond.* She is also the founder and editor of *laJoie, The Journal in Appreciation of All Animals.*

"Pet owners are never at a loss for humor and laughter . . . "

"What time does the petting zoo open?"

Introduction

If I were to be asked to describe my story in a single word, that word would be "symbiosis," the intimate living together of dissimilar organisms in a mutually beneficial relationship. This is the story of the symbiotic relationships between a married couple (the author and his wife) and our animals—dogs, cats, and, last but certainly in no way least, horses. All of the animals fulfilled many deep needs in us and we in them. We benefited each other. We cherished each other. We rescued one another. And I often ask myself: Did these creatures come into our lives because we needed them or did it only seem that way?

And our animals and their people are definitely dissimilar organisms! As I daily remind myself, dogs and cats are NOT small, silent people in fur coats! Horses are NOT large, hoofed people in leather coats!

Let me name our animal companions now and, in the pages that follow, tell you all about them and how we all came to serve (and save) one another later.

First was Cuddles, a mostly white Cockapoo and a tiny rag mop of a dog, with whom Connie and I began our marriage in 1975.

Next came Gus, a platinum Poodle, who joined us when we moved from Delaware to California six months later.

After Cuddles' death nine years later, we added Duffy, a West Highland White Terrier from a pet store.

When Gus died after twenty years with us, we found a black Scottish Terrier at a local animal shelter and named her Katie Scarlet (after the heroine in *Gone with the Wind*).

Then my wife got a yen for a Himalayan cat and we bought a kitten and christened her Ana-purr-na, a.k.a. Purr. She is beautiful—with blue eyes and masses of long tawny hair.

Four years ago, after twenty-three years of suburban existence, we moved to the country where we have three majestically scruffy acres of land that include a two-stall stable, a sanded arena, and an acre or so of pasture. But before we located a horse, we were convinced that we needed a "barn cat" to live in our hay room to discourage the mice as well as a "real dog" to wander our acreage.

A classified ad led me three miles from our home to a young man who was leaving for college and could not take his six-week-old Queensland Heeler puppy with him. The dog's half-black and half-white face intrigued me and I bought her. We named her "Nehi"—not because of the chocolate soft drink of our childhood but because she was only "knee high to a grasshopper" then and because we expected her to be about "knee high" to us at maturity.

My wife's cousin's best friend, who is the local unofficial full-time animal rescuer, brought us a downtrodden, wounded, abused, and starved black cat with a cauliflower ear and shaved areas on her body where she had undergone recent surgeries. She had also survived a shooting attempt. I named her "Cat-tas-strophe," "Tassy" for short. But she preferred "Barn Cat" or "Blackie" or even "BC." Our plan was to have Tassy live in the tack room of our stable to deal with the field mice and restrict our expensive fuzz ball of a Himalayan to the house. Connie was sure that she was raising a lap cat of her own.

After a few weeks of regular meals, Tassy fattened up so much that our vet and we were sure she was pregnant. Fearing that she would have kittens in some inaccessible place on the property such as under our deck, we kept her in the tack room 24/7. We made sure that she had plenty of food and water and that she was visited regularly. More weeks went by. No kittens. So we released her from confinement.

As Purr grew to adulthood, she decided that she is my cat and nobody else's. She comes to me frequently every day for brushing and just to snuggle in my lap. Sometimes she sleeps on my pillow but usually, regardless of the weather, she spends the night outdoors, patrolling the grounds.

Cat-tas-strophe

TASSY

"Good morning. I'm a lawyer
representing the family of
the mouse that Tassy ate!"

Despite her pampered appearance, she is not an indoor cat. She prefers to slink around our front and back yards, hiding in the shrubs, and stalking birds.

Lest Connie feel rejected, she was adopted by Tassy, who accompanied her everywhere, indoors and out, and frequently used Connie as her personal furniture, although her favorite place was the back of the sofa where Connie read, watched TV, or reclined. Also, Tassy knew a magic trick that kept Connie amazed and amused. She did not follow Connie as much as she materialized a few feet ahead of her, no matter where on our property my wife went. And she was deadly to the mice. (Connie was glad to see the mouse population depleted but was upset by the fact that Tassy ate the creatures as soon as she dispatched them. *Crunch, crunch, crunch!*)

"This one is for Best in Show, and
this one is for pulling Stormy off the judges!"

We had purchased our new home because of its equine accommodations—my wife had wanted a horse of her own since childhood. She sought a paint horse and a huge brown and white mare came up for sale in our town. It was advertised in our local all-ads newspaper and I was the first of more than twenty who phoned the day the notice appeared. This gave Connie first right of refusal, which she never considered. So Stormy became my wife's horse.

A year later, as Connie was making slow but steady progress with the care and nurture of the BIG GIRL (her shoulders are higher than my wife is tall!) and was riding with some slight degree of confidence, I decided that I would like a horse of my own so that we could take trail rides together. Accompanied by an experienced horseman we knew from the paint horse organization, we looked at every horse that seemed suited to my needs in a three-county area. Sheer exhaustion prompted our friend to offer us a red roan and white paint gelding he had gotten in a trade. And so I bought a horse with the unwieldy name of "Sur-bourbon-on-the-rocks" and dubbed him "Ragtime Cow Horse Joe," which was shortened to the simpler "Rags." (Just try hailing a horse named "Sur-bourbon-on-the-rocks"—especially when one is an ordained minister who is a teetotaler!)

Ragtime Cow Horse Joe
RAGS

Forty years ago, when my daughter Susan was about three, she sang incessantly and somewhat incorrectly about "Puff the Magic Shragon." I remember the line, "A dragon lives forever, but not so little boys." And even though any given pet will be there for a large fraction of one's life, they are no more everlasting than little Jackie Paper, Puff's playmate.

After all, dogs and cats age at about seven times the rate of humans. While I was at work on this book, two of our beloved companions—Duffy and Tassy—died. Duffy was an old man of almost fourteen and Tassy of undetermined age. Connie decided that the remaining two dogs, one cat, and two horses were "more than enough," but then we met Rizzi, a tricolor Queensland Heeler who had been found at the scene of a hellacious forest fire at an Indian reservation. And so our family changes . . . .

If I had to choose just one word to describe each animal, I would call him or her:

Cuddles the dancer
Gus the lover
Duffy the protector
Katie the obdurate
Nehi the tireless
Purr the empress
Tassy the ubiquitous
Stormy the mighty
Rags the beloved
Rizzi the charismatic

RON

"Hey, I was just thinking, can we get an orangutan?"

Cuddles the Dancer

Connie and I were living in an apartment in Wilmington, Delaware, just after our marriage in 1975. We were on the verge of moving to our first owned residence, a small row house, in Newark, Delaware, a half hour's drive away. Meanwhile, we were trying our best to improve our respective relationships with our children from our first marriages. My son and daughter lived nearby with their mother in suburban Wilmington and Connie's sons were visiting with their father in California. They were supposed to rejoin us when the school year began and I was apprehensive about my new role as a stepfather.

As we were window-shopping at a suburban mall one evening, we passed a pet shop where Connie noticed a Cockapoo. Not then a recognized breed, Cockapoos are a cross between Cocker Spaniels and Poodles. Connie declared that she had always wanted one of these cute little critters. So the next day, I phoned the Wilmington Humane Society and asked if a Cockapoo were available for adoption. "It's strange that you should ask," I was told. "We never have them but right now we have a female that has been abandoned by her owner."

After work that day, we drove to the shelter and were introduced to "Cuddles," a two-year-old female. An attendant opened a large dog carrier and there, huddled in the back, was a trembling, dirty, matted mass of hair surrounding a tiny dog. She looked like the aftermath of an explosion at a sweater factory. Cuddles resisted when the attendant tried to remove her, was finally lifted from the carrier, and proceeded to pee all over the attendant's uniform. We didn't think much of her but we agreed to take her on a trial basis. The paperwork stated that a family had abandoned the dog because she was "a biter." These were not good signs!

Connie attempted to walk Cuddles on a lead but the dog kept seeking large objects to hide behind. When we took her out into the parking lot, she repeatedly scooted under automobiles to find sanctuary behind their tires. Even so, Connie decided that we would take the huddled mass on a trial basis. (I know now that there is no such thing. Owners may fail their trials but pets never do!)

When we got her to our apartment, I bathed her and attempted without success to detangle her coat. I offered her canned dog food in a small bowl and she refused it, scooting over to our sofa and snuggling against it. The terrified little animal did not seem to know how to walk on a leash or how to eat out of a dog dish. For the first few days, I sat on the floor next to her and fed her with a spoon. Her only daily activity was to scrunch up against our living room sofa, totally ignoring us. She never left that sofa unless I carried her outside for a walk. Connie lamented to me, "I am convinced that this dog has no personality! We should take her back to the shelter."

This pattern continued for several days. Then, one night, while I attended a meeting of my board of directors, Connie was in the back bedroom of our apartment, ironing clothes. Cuddles was huddled in her usual place about forty feet away. Suddenly Connie heard the sound of scurrying feet and the little dog appeared before her, standing on her back legs and dancing. The performance was repeated for me when I returned and it became a daily event for months to come. "Cuddles has decided to keep us," I surmised. She began eating from her dog dish and, true to her name, spent every evening cuddling up to one of us on the sofa as we watched television.

During the nine years we spent together, she never bit anyone although she would growl and snap at any male who approached her in a loud, animated manner. She was a sweetheart who would dance for any audience upon request.

She was a comfort to both of us as we faced many personal challenges during the months ahead. Without warning, I learned from the morning newspaper that I was being investigated by a Grand Jury, the FBI, the IRS, postal authorities, and (or so it seemed) whoever else felt like jumping on the bandwagon. Though I was never indicted of anything, the suspicions raised destroyed most of my Delaware friendships as well as my relationship with my board of directors and with my community contacts. Our limited savings were exhausted by legal fees. (It was the early post-Watergate era. And folks in positions of community leadership—I had been responsible for a successful and well-publicized crusade against a decrepit and inhumane mental health treatment system in Delaware—were fair game for ambitious prosecutors.)

"I think Cuddles must have heard you
telling me she has no personality!"

We moved into our new home in Newark but would only be there for a few weeks. There was no way I could keep my job. Meanwhile, my wife's ex-husband offered to keep the boys with him until we completed our move but, along the way, he and the boys decided that they wanted to remain together in California.

Since it was impossible for Connie to maintain any semblance of a normal relationship with her sons unless we relocated near them, I began applying for jobs in California. After two scouting trips to California, the Mental Association in San Mateo County—the county in which the San Francisco Airport is located—hired me.

So we packed up again, placed our goods on a moving van, and flew with Cuddles to California to begin a new life. I was so happy to leave behind the unpalatable distractions of my Delaware existence and to move to the land of my childhood dreams that I cried on the plane.

We rented a small, craftsman-style bungalow with two bedrooms and one bathroom not far from the airport in Burlingame. The moving company lost our furniture for two weeks and when it finally arrived the movers demanded twice their original estimate. I began my new job in January of 1976 and Connie found a secretarial job at a real estate firm.

Every day, amid all the confusion, disruptions, and changes in our lives, our little dog danced for us and cuddled next to us. (Whoever had previously owned her had certainly named her well!)

Whenever Connie and I were going to be away from home at the same time, we made arrangements for Cuddles to travel with us. The choice of motels that allow pets is somewhat limited. Cuddles was on her best behavior and caused no problems. With my son and daughter still in Delaware or away at college and Connie's sons with their father on weekdays during the school year, I guess Cuddles was our child substitute. Every bit of affection and attention we lavished on her was returned to us many times over.

Cuddles had a skin condition that required regular doses of an anti-inflammatory drug. No matter what technique I used, the little dog would spit out the pill. When we were staying at a motel in Monterey, I brought the remnants of a steak dinner to the room and cut a slit into a juicy morsel and hid the pill in it. I fed her a few small pieces of the steak and then the one in which the pill was buried. She chewed the meat, found the pill with her tongue, walked over to me and deposited it on my foot!

In 1976, our first year in California, Connie prepared for her sons the usual Easter baskets with decorated eggs, jelly beans, and candy bunnies. The piece de resistance was a boxed hollow chocolate rabbit with a blue satin bow around its neck. Matt, the eight-year-old, was hoarding his for some future occasion. While we were all out for the day, it disappeared. Connie and I had an Early American bed with a mattress that stood at about waist height. There, in the middle of the bed, was the cardboard box, its cellophane wrapper neatly removed, the box open and sliced, and the ribbon bow sitting empty. It was as though someone had opened the box with a razor blade, eaten the chocolate bunny, and placed the evidence in perfect order!

No doubt, Cuddles was the perpetrator. But how had this little animal gotten into Matt's bed, dragged the candy box to our bedroom, jumped onto our bed with the box, and opened it? As far as we knew, Cuddles had never jumped even half the height of our mattress.

Cuddles the Traveler

Cuddles was the best traveled of our pets. I have already mentioned how she danced her way into our hearts and of her first airplane trip to California. Just before that journey, the three of us had moved to our new (and very temporary) home in Newark and I decided that the time had come to try to do something about her densely matted coat. I made an appointment with a groomer, asking her to leave as much fur as possible. When I returned to the groomer, Cuddles had been totally denuded down to the skin. The only fur remaining was at the end of her tail. Minus all her tangled and disheveled mane, Cuddles looked like a large, spotted Mexican hairless.

Connie and I were scheduled to attend a conference in San Diego, California. Since we knew no one in Newark, we decided to take the bald little dog with us. We bought an appropriate carrier, stocked it with food and water, received assurances from the airline that the dog would be placed in a secure, heated compartment, and flew off to California. When we arrived at our destination, we were horrified to

"These pills don't seem to be doing Cuddles any good!"

discover the water in her carrier frozen into a solid block and our Cuddles in much the same condition.

How our furless traveler survived is still a mystery. She was chilled to the bone but otherwise fine.

A few days later, we were on our way back to Delaware, and the airline did a better job for us. Within a month, I was offered my new position and we were once again en route from Delaware to the West Coast—Cuddles flying for the third time in a month.

For years, our trips with Cuddles were by car until she developed a dental problem, the treatment for which was simply beyond our means. It turned out that it would be cheaper to fly to Idaho, where Connie's sister Norma lived, and have Cuddles treated at the animal clinic where Norma worked. Country vets charge much less than their big city counterparts, especially when the country vet in question happens to be your wife's brother-in-law-to-be. We retrieved the long unused pet carrier from the garage, reassembled it, and once again, packed Cuddles for transit, having first secured the state required health certification. By now, several years after her earlier hairless

In later years, Cuddles wasn't as
energetic as she used to be.

ordeals, Cuddles had a finely tended full coat, the proper walking dust mop look!

So off Cuddles and I went. She was remarkably cooperative, sitting patiently during the procedure, requiring no anesthesia. And the veteran animal doctor reported that she was "excellent company" at his clinic.

The treatment was successful and either the fresh air or the blend of farm animal odors at Norma's ranch seemed to breathe new life into the aging dog. Cuddles would run excitedly from place to place, dash up to one of her people to share a moment of excited affection, and then run some more. Then she terrified me by tunneling under the foundation of Norma's farmhouse and disappearing, only to reemerge in a few minutes, looking like a matron pulling off an overly tight girdle.

I expressed my amazement at Cuddles' rejuvenation, but sage Norma opined, "It's no surprise. That's what country living does for animals—and for people, too!" Little did I know that such revitalization through rural existence awaited me twenty years in the future.

Other than stealing chocolate bunnies, Cuddles had one other bad trait. When she was left alone while Connie and I were at work, she would wet one of our rugs. Connie's conclusion was that she was lonely and we should find her a companion "to keep her company." Thus cometh Gus!

Gus the Lover

The ad said, "Cockapoo. Free to good home." We phoned the owner and when we returned home from work, a red British sports car with a license plate reading, "DOG," was sitting in front of our house. Before we saw the owner or the dog, Connie cautioned me, "He'll never let us have his dog. He's named his car after it."

In came Dick, a short man with red hair and a matching mous-
tache, and Gus, who I can only describe as a heap of silver gray, kinky
hair. Dick had owned Gus for about two years and let him run loose
in the morning to follow the joggers in his neighborhood. Dick obviously loved this energetic rascal of a dog but his girlfriend did not.
Plus they were on their way to Mexico and could not take a dog along.

Dick interviewed us for nearly an hour as though he were a social
worker placing a special-needs child and decided that we could offer
Gus a good home. So with a tear in his eye, he climbed into his little
convertible and drove away.

Gus inspected every room of our house as well as the backyard
and tried to buddy up with Cuddles. But she studiously avoided him.

A few days later, I bought a dog-grooming clipper and attempted to remove some of Gus's tangle of hair. It was like cutting steel
wool with a pair of plastic scissors. Off to Erskine, the overly affectionate groomer, we went, and after he had worked his magic, much

RON

"You can't plead 'insanity' for
failing to scoop the poop!"

to our amazement, we discovered not a cockapoo but a platinum Poodle with an undocked tail under all that tangled mess. He definitely had a Poodle head but long legs, cottony silver and gray hair, a long tail, and, above all, his eyes—large, brown, expressive, and more humanlike than canine—made us wonder just what he really was.

Gus was unneutered and an escape artist. No matter where we secured him, indoors or out, he would tunnel under a fence or squeeze through a partially opened window and disappear, only to return a short time later leading a female dog, always a purebred. His taste was eclectic. His amorata included a tiny dachshund, a Sheltie, a Samoyed, and a klutzy Newfoundland. (To mate with her, he would have needed a stepladder! I suggested he had "high hopes.")

Not once did an owner show up to claim his female dog or to complain to us about Gus's wanderings. Many owners simply let their dogs wander about during the day, much as Gus had accustomed himself to doing against our every effort. The only time we were ever reprimanded for a leashless pet was quite strange—a man was walking by our house with an unleashed male dog. Connie and Cuddles were sitting together in the living room, looking out a partially opened window. When the passerby saw Cuddles, he shouted, "Lady, keep your bitch under control." Connie shot back, "She's not a bitch. She's been spayed." Apparently his dog owner's manual informed him that male dogs could wander at will, but that girl dogs should be locked up. Thus, among dog owners, male chauvinist sexism rears its ugly head!

"Cuddles was right, these convenience foods are quite tasty!"

Prior to Gus's arrival on the scene, I had tried to teach Cuddles to fetch. She showed absolutely no interest. For Gus, however, retrieving anything thrown—wads of paper, sticks, dog biscuits, or balls—was second nature. His skill and enthusiasm for bounced tennis balls somehow aroused jealousy in Cuddles, and she insisted in joining the game! Since his legs were much longer than hers, there was no way that she could beat him to the object of pursuit, so I would have to restrain him to give her a head start. Fetch did not improve the relationship between Gus and Cuddles, however—daily he tried to befriend her but she continued to spurn him.

Gus was as skillful a thief as Cuddles. His favorite booty was pumpkin pie. If we left a freshly baked pie to cool on our butcher block or range top, he would stretch those long legs of his to the surface and with his tongue scoop out a moat around the outer edge of the pie. When we placed pies away from such easy-to-reach places, he would jump to almost any surface in the house and dig his trench.

Now I had my odd couple, the white dust mop and the gray whatever, to walk morning and evening. I was a bad neighbor, I must admit, not yet having learned the etiquette of poop scooping. The old bungalows on my one-block circle route had small front yards, sidewalks, and small buffers of grass between the curb and the sidewalk. That's where I walked the dogs, as did other neighborhood dog owners.

Gus was as affectionate and as snuggly as Cuddles. First, Cuddles would choose a lap, usually Connie's, and then Gus would sidle up to me and place his head on my leg. Cuddles preferred quiet, restrained people, usually women, while Gus was everyone's friend. If you placed your arms in front of you with your palms turned upwards, he would jump into your arms. He was especially devoted to my older stepson, Todd. They played their own version of the leaping game for years. Even when grown up and his work schedule as a sheriff's deputy permitted him to visit us, Todd would tap his shoulders with his fingertips and say, "jump," and Gus would trustingly spring up into empty air, confident that Todd would catch him.

After a year, we moved to another rental home, this time in nearby Foster City, a planned community with parks, canals, a lagoon for sailboats and canoes, shopping centers, schools, and miles of San Francisco Bay frontage. A wide spot in one of the canals with a sandy beach was right out the front door of our contemporary cottage.

"Nice going, Gus. I just wrote in my diary
that you never caught any!"

In Burlingame, everything had been old and worn. The old swing-out windows lacked screens or locks. In Foster City, everything was new and modern. The windows locked and had screens, storm windows, and mini-blinds. But the wooden-fenced backyard was a desert of sand and silt—Foster City was built on reclaimed swampland filled with Bay-bottom sediment.

My new neighbors in our cul-de-sac quickly educated me to the need to clean up after my dogs when I walked them. To avoid this messy chore, I took to crossing the street behind our house where there was nothing but a square mile of undeveloped fill land, bounded by a major canal or slough, on the other side of which was Marine World Africa USA. (Every evening the roar of the hungry lions and tigers demanding their meals seemed to be coming from just outside our dining room windows.) In this vast wasteland, I would set Gus free to run in pursuit of jackrabbits, with him the whole time baying in a high-pitched screech that sounded as though he were in pain. Connie recalls, "I could tell where he was by the baying, and occasionally I could see his head popping up over the weeds and his long ears flopping up and down." He could keep on the trail of a rabbit for half a mile, always within a few feet of his prey but never catching it, and then immediately return at breakneck speed to my side, not even breathing heavily.

Gus was a superb mouser. With great pride, he would hunt down field mice on our property and bring us their remains. Early one morning as we were awakening, one of his intended victims jumped up into our bed and ran across my wife's head and my pillow. Another time, he pursued a terrified mouse into the end of a fifteen-foot masonry drainpipe in the backyard. The creature scooted out the back end while Gus sat patiently at the front waiting stoically for it to emerge, never realizing that it was gone. For days afterwards, he would go to the same spot and wait for that elusive mouse!

I sometimes let the dogs off their leads at the beach where they would scatter the seagulls and then run along the shoreline coping of the canal to a bridge leading to the next subdivision. However, this proved to be a bad idea for two reasons. One day, as Cuddles raced on her short legs to keep pace with Gus, he bounded from the coping to the bridge. When she tried to follow, she landed in the canal and scratched frantically at the banks without being able to climb out. Connie, her high heels sinking into the silt, dashed madly after Cuddles, pulling the soaking wet animal to safety. This obviously was not a safe place for the little white dog. Also, I was violating the local leash law—a fact to which I became educated when a bird-loving neighbor reported me to the police. So from then on, I either walked the dogs on leads or took them to the undeveloped open fields.

In our new home in Foster City, Cuddles was her mostly sedentary, affectionate, entertaining self. Gus, on the other hand, remained true to his more adventuresome nature. One Saturday morning, he tunneled his way beneath a side fence in our backyard and woke us by bringing a retinue of female dogs into our bed. Another time, he pulled his Houdini act and roamed until found by animal control more than a mile from our home. And then there was the unforgettable holiday weekend we visited Connie's parents in Davis, California, and he slipped his leash and went off in pursuit of a pair of German Shepherds. He slunk back in minutes, his head down, his tail between his legs. The big dogs had attacked him, puncturing his lower backside in several places. Fortunately for him, Davis is the home of a major veterinary school. We rushed him there and he was sewn back together. Not giving us time to say that we were already in Davis when Gus was injured, they looked at our home address on their forms and expressed amazement: "You brought him all the way from the Bay area!" (a more than two-hour drive).

The time had come to have Gus fixed. Back at home, I secured him and phoned the SPCA for an appointment, which was scheduled for the next day. That night, he scratched his way through an aluminum window screen, tunneled under a concrete fence foundation, and was once again found by animal control, this time treading water feebly in a canal. (Did he know what lay ahead for him? Was he depressed at the thought? Had he tried to end it all? Or was he only trying to escape?)

The operation proceeded.

There would be no more visits from his honeys.

"Oh yeah? Well *my* dog can *talk*,
but the dog food companies
are paying us to keep quiet!"

Gus "Speaks"!

Dog owners are true believers. Their faith in their ability to intuit their canine companion's inner life is boundless. They are prone to projection, to say the least. They imagine that their pets are bombarding them with all sorts of messages and clues; they read into their pets' whines, barks, tail twitches, patterns of behavior—both usual and unusual—all sorts of communications. How many of these actions are our pets speaking to us and how many of them are mere figments of our imaginations and emotional neediness no one can say. So it was with Gus and me.

When we lived on San Miguel in Foster City, I would generally be the first one home from work. When I came home, Gus would be sitting in the doorway, head held high, chest expanded, tail wagging, and an alert and focused expression on his face. And he would say, "Hello, Lowell!"—or so it sounded to me. It's possible he was just moaning something like, "Woe-oh-woe," but it sure sounded like a very personal salutation to me. Further, he never greeted anyone else in this manner, which, of course meant that no one ever believed me when I reported the matter to family and friends. Did that make any difference to me? Not in the least.

Gus was not our only "speaking" dog. Later, our Westie, Duffy, would demonstrate a very different way of communicating, using a combination of growls, yowls, grunts, body movements, and barks. I am sure that he spoke whole sentences! Once as I was reading in the living room at the front of the house, he broke into a particular warning that went something like this: "O OU WOO O WOO WOO!" After repeating this a few times with sudden movements in the direction of the kitchen, he became impatient with  me for not understanding him and ran out the dog door in the kitchen and confronted a pair of raccoons that were feasting on a loaf of bread they had removed from our breadbox! Duffy growled and snapped until

23

the bandits ran away. Since the raccoons not only outnumbered him but also were each about twice his size and notoriously savage, Duffy's actions merited a medal for valor—the *coeur de cur*! After this event, I paid close attention whenever he raised the alarm, "O OU WOO O WOO WOO!"

Cuddles and Gus on Gull Avenue

1979 was a year of changes. Connie's father died and her mother came to live with us. I turned forty. (I invited several new acquaintances from the local Rotary Club to my birthday party—most brought bottles of Scotch. I don't drink! Twenty-five years later, I still have some of the liquor.) I also began a new job.

A few months earlier, in November of 1978, I was invited to accompany my congressman, Leo Ryan, on his fact-finding mission to the Peoples Temple compound in Guyana. By the time the invitation reached me, it was too late for me to join the Ryan party. After the mass suicide/murder at Jonestown and the murder of Ryan, I resigned my post with the Mental Health Association and was named executive director of the Human Freedom Center in Berkeley, a one-hour drive from Foster City. The Human Freedom Center provided shelter and reassurance to survivors of the massacre, to family members of victims as well as to former members of Peoples Temple. The Center also began to offer information and counseling services to individuals and families whose lives had been disrupted by other high-demands religious groups.

Cuddles and "Mom" (Betty Johnson, Connie's mother) became a team. Mom would sit reading or working on her never-ending needlepoint or crocheting projects in an easy chair she had brought with her from her home in Davis, California, and Cuddles would jump into her lap and settle into a comfortable spot beside her.

Gus no longer pursued rabbits or bitches. He seemed content stalking leftovers, especially cakes and pies, that had not been promptly put away. Betty and Connie worked together in a secretarial services business

Connie had started, and I was either away for the day in Berkeley or traveling to various parts of the United States, Canada, or Europe, helping to reunite families that had been torn asunder by religious differences. So Cuddles and Gus had free run of the house until dinnertime. Now and then, one of them would get into mischief—spill a vase of flowers, pull afghans or blankets from beds or furniture, or soil a carpet. When I came in, I would demand, "WHO DID THIS?" and Gus would always confess, placing his head between his paws, his soulful, humanlike brown eyes downcast, his body trembling from end to end, whether he was guilty or not! (Cuddles was totally unmoved by my anger.)

Sometimes he was as guilty as Bill Clinton. He would jump up on our dining room table and pee on the centerpiece or bend the slats on the huge mini-blinds that covered the patio sliding door so that he could improve his view of the backyard.

In 1980, we bought our first California home, a long, narrow, stucco-covered, shake-roofed ranch house with five bedrooms and two bathrooms on Gull Avenue in Foster City. There was a pleasant fenced backyard with a wooden deck, climbing roses, trees, shrubbery, and a lawn. I installed a pet door so the dogs could come and go as they pleased. Out the front door, six houses to the left, were a tidy park, playground, and lagoon complete with a sandy beach. Every morning, I would walk the dogs there before I left for work.

Later, when I walked the same route with Katie and Duffy, pedestrians my age or older would marvel at the paired Scottie and Westie, asking me if I were advertising for Buchanan's Black and White Blended Whiskey. (Remember those ads?) One local insisted that I should have named them "Scotch and Soda." Middle-aged or younger folk do not recall the Black and White logo any more than they remember Pearl Harbor! And when they today ask me if I have a Scotty to be like the President, they are thinking of George W. Bush and Barney rather than FDR and Fala!

In neighboring San Mateo, one of the main drags bears the name given to it centuries ago by Franciscan monks, Alameda de las Pulgas, "avenue of the fleas." Nearly five hundred years later, those bloodsuckers still rule the region. Flea powders, sprays, dips, collars—none of them of great efficacy—were as much a regular part of our budget as bread and milk. With her irritable skin, Cuddles was particularly

"It's a note from that Sunday School teacher
who lives next door, asking us to pull the blinds!"

molested by the parasites. Often while Betty worked on her needle-point, I would spend the evening picking the detestable creatures from Cuddles' skin and crushing them one at a time. Once a week, I took both dogs into our bathtub, got in with them, and shampooed them carefully, insuring that they would have only clean fleas. Both dogs were patient as I bathed them, held them up to the showerhead to rinse them, and toweled them off.

During a family get-together at our home, Jason, my pre-teenage nephew, asked if he could take Gus for a walk. I put Gus on a leash and directed the boy and the dog to the little park down the street. Jason decided that it would be fun to watch Gus run loose in the park. Unfortunately, Gus headed directly for the lagoon, and when boy and dog returned to our house, Gus was soaked in oily, brackish water. I sternly admonished Jason that it would be his responsibility to bathe Gus. His reaction was rather like that of Prissy in *Gone with the Wind:* "I don't know nothing 'bout washing no dogs."

I explained that bathing a dog is not very different from sham-pooing one's own head, led boy and dog to the bathroom, turned on the water, and presented Jason with a bottle of dog shampoo. He was a quick study. Today Jason is a talented computer programmer and the father of two. He still, however, with a muted expression of out-rage, brings up the matter of having to shampoo our dog!

Gus was a swimmer. There was no question about it. On another occasion, we were picnicking at a state park on the Bay. Matt, Connie's younger son, picked up a six-inch-long piece of driftwood that lay on the beach, and threw it into the Bay. Gus was away like a shot, splashing into the waves, paddling skillfully, and returning with the wood in his mouth.

Cuddles was our cotton dog; she would probably have sunk into the water. Gus seemed to be covered with something more water-resistant, rather like a Scotchgarded shag rug.

Competing with Gus, Cuddles became a skilled tennis ball retriever. We would go to the little park and I would hold one of them on a lead, while the other chased the ball. Although unable to outrun the rabbit-legged Gus, Cuddles was remarkably speedy in her own right. One day, I threw the ball and she pursued it, but this time some wild ducks at the water's edge distracted her. She swiftly detoured after them and abruptly stepped into a hole, injuring one of her back legs.

She was unable to walk, so I lifted her in my arms and carried her home. The next day, our kindly veterinarian informed us that she had the same type of knee injury often suffered by football players and that she would need an expensive operation. When owner and pet are mutually devoted, health care is not optional.

After the surgery, there was a long convalescent period. Cuddles was in a cast and every morning I carried her to the park where she preferred to complete her bodily functions. (There was a scruffy, bushy area where no humans ever set foot that was her favorite lavatory spot. Ironically, it was behind a long abandoned public toilet.)

As Cuddles aged, she lost interest in pursuit games and turned her ball-fetching responsibilities over to the swifter Gus. Because of her injury and surgery, she no longer volunteered to dance and we no longer requested that she did. She still relished our morning walks, however. In the evenings, she divided her time between Betty and

RON

"Now you can look at my bill!"

Connie, tightly snuggling up with one or the other while Gus was on the sofa with me, his head in my lap.

One morning, when she was about eleven, Cuddles refused my urgings to join for our walk. I tugged and pulled on her leash but she would not budge. I carried her outside and tried again. Still no response. A quick trip to the vet revealed that she had an inoperable abdominal tumor. Before saying my goodbyes, I tried to engage her, to thank her out loud for having been such a "good dog" and having brought us such joy during our years together. But her mind was elsewhere. An assistant opened a door to come to fetch her and she turned toward the light as it entered the room. Then she was gone.

I cried every morning for weeks at her loss—more than I ever had wept for the loss of anyone close to me who had died. I was desolate. This was the first time in my life that I had to cope with the loss of a pet.

Every morning as I walked Gus, neighbors would inquire about the rag mop dog. When I told them of her death, they would ask me if Gus missed her. "I'll bet he's lonesome," they would say. I guess I will never know. They had never been close, never played together or interacted, never fought over food or for their owners' attention. Cuddles' attitude had always seemed to be, "A dog! You expect me to associate with a *dog*?"

And Gus? Well, he simply kept on keeping on.

Our pets live relatively short lives. For many of us who love our pets, their death can affect some of us even more than the death of a relative or friend. The death of a pet leaves few people totally untouched. A pet may come to symbolize many things to each of us. It may represent a child, perhaps a child yet to be conceived or the innocent child in us all. It may reflect the ideal mate or parent, ever faithful, patient and welcoming, loving us unconditionally. It is a playmate and a sibling. It is a reflection of ourselves, embodying negative and positive qualities we recognize or lack in ourselves. The same pet may be all of these, alternating between roles on any given day or for each member of the family.

The "Healing" of Gus

> If I have any beliefs about immortality, it is that certain dogs
> I have known will go to heaven, and very, very few persons.
> —James Thurber

[I wrote the following at our home in Foster City, California, in 1993.]

Gus is my twenty-year-old platinum poodle. Gus has been a member of our family since shortly after Connie and I married. He is very precious to us—even though he can no longer jump five feet into our extended arms, or run down rodents, or stand on his hind legs and steal food off the kitchen table, or tunnel under fences to keep romantic trysts with canine girl-friends several times his size and weight, later bringing them home to meet his people.

Nevertheless, Gus is still Gus—the paradigm of unconditional, affectionate companionship. I would find it strange to read a newspaper without his head in my lap or write a sermon without him napping at my feet. (He must have overheard my thoughts. He just pulled himself to his feet and walked away, only to return a minute later with our other dog, Duffy, a four-year-old West Highland White Terrier.)

As I was saying, Gus naps—after the exhilaration he evidences when let out into the backyard and fed his dog biscuits, that's what Gus does most of the time, he naps. You see, Gus is a dog in retirement. As befits his senior citizen status, Gus suffers from arthritis, cataracts, and partial deafness. So I have tried to prepare myself for his inevitable passing. Twenty years is a considerable age even for one with Gus's zest for life.

About two years ago, I experienced one of the most harrowing weeks of my life. On a Thursday morning, as Connie prepared to leave for a business trip of several days' duration, she noticed that Gus was ill. He had lost his dinner, had become disoriented, and could

"Being as I don't know what's wrong with her,
I'll only charge you two hundred dollars!"

scarcely walk. Moreover, his head hung at a strange angle, as though it were not connected to his body. I rushed him to the animal hospital and was told, after many anxious hours, that he had an "idiopathic condition." "Idiopathic condition"—I think that's Greek for "God only knows!" The prognosis was not good. Even if he survived, I was told, it was unlikely that he would ever return to normal.

For six days and nights, Gus was on life support—IV's and catheters keeping him alive. His condition worsened by the day and

**"I just read your book and I can tell
you for a fact that God didn't think
you were being selfish when you prayed for Gus!"**

the bills mounted alarmingly. Those close to me advised that I put
him to sleep. Over the weekend, he had been transferred to an even
more expensive emergency hospital, where visitors were not allowed.

On Monday morning, when I was able to see him, he tried to
stand and walk over to me, but could not. He raised his chin—his signal that he wanted to be petted. That was all he could manage.

I arrived Tuesday, expecting to be with him for the last time. I had
brought his collar and leash so that I could leave them with the vet to
be disposed of. I was led to the room where he was caged and asked if
I could be left alone with him to bid him farewell. I opened the door to

his kennel. There was no reaction. An open, sad, imploring eye was the only sign of life. I talked to him, pleaded with him, and cried over him.

And then I prayed aloud. I said something like this: "God, I don't know if it's proper for me to pray for my dog. It seems selfish somehow. But he is a wonderful friend and I wonder if you could find it in your heart to give him back to me for just a little while. I'm not ready to say goodbye to him just yet. I need him."

Suddenly Gus began trembling as he pushed his front elbows into the kennel floor. In a few seconds he was on his feet. His head listing bizarrely to one side, he shambled and slid toward me, his muzzle lifted to receive a pat on the head.

An hour later, he walked for the first time in a week. He began eating and drinking again. Other functions returned. He was weak and unsteady, but definitely on the mend. A day later, the amazed and delighted veterinarian asked me to take him home. "Come and get him," the vet said. "He's eating like a pig!" (A week later, he was better than he had been before the illness. Two years later, older, frailer, and stiffer in the joints, he hangs in there. We call him "the Energizer dog" because he keeps going, and going, and going. When I take him to the vet, members of the staff gather to greet him. They exclaim, "Look, it's Gus, Gus, the amazing Gus!")

One thing for sure—Gus's recovery was a faith healing. The only question is: whose faith, his or mine?

[I added the following update at our new home in Cottonwood, California, in 2002.]

I needed Gus more than I realized. Unknown to me at the time, I was suffering from two unrelated forms of cancer (colon and kidney) and diabetes. Gus lived to be twenty-three, the oldest dog ever seen in our veterinarian's practice. He comforted me through two major surgeries, debilitating chemotherapy, the loss of my job as congregational pastor, and postoperative and post-church depression. The colon cancer had spread into my lymph nodes. I was told that I had two years to live. That was nine years ago. You see, I had a guardian angel—that's what animal companions are, messengers of the grace of God. I had a guardian angel named "Gus" to distract me from worry, to make me feel loved and needed, to urge me to get up and go for walks, and to make me laugh. Thank you, Gus. Thank you, Lord, for Gus.

Duffy the Protector

After the death of Cuddles, Connie and I began discussing the option of adopting another dog. We were ambivalent. Most pets die during their owners' lifetimes. Wasn't the sorrow of losing Cuddles enough? And there were practical considerations. After all, it's much easier to maintain one dog than two, but it is lonelier—for both pet and owner.

On a visit to a nearby shopping mall pet store, we encountered a tiny puppy, a West Highland White Terrier. Connie loved the active little dog but she was opposed to our buying him. Her reasons:

(1) The high cost. The pet store was asking $500 for a "puppy mill" dog.
(2) The little dog was a male and Connie was concerned that Gus would not accept him.
(3) The puppy was far from show quality. He had a thin coat and a strange twist at the base of his tail, a genetic defect.

For six months, Connie found every excuse to visit the pet store and play with the lively little guy. He would scamper from one end of the sizeable shop to the other, sometimes alone and sometimes accompanied by an adult Westie belonging to a clerk who worked at the shop. The little dog would delight Connie by sitting on his rump and stretching his head and front legs in the air—a characteristic Westie begging maneuver.

Connie named the dog "Duffy." Once, Connie became so enchanted by the pup that she forgot we were on our way to the airport to pick up my daughter, whom we kept waiting for nearly an hour.

August 1, our fourteenth wedding anniversary was approaching, and I decided to go in search of Duffy as an appropriate gift. Fortunately, he had not been sold yet and a moment of dickering

"Of course West Highland Terriers are expensive.
They're very rare you know!"

lowered his price to $250. (While I bargained with the pet store man-
ager, the little dog emptied a complete box of Kleenex, one tissue at a
time, and shredded them at my feet!)

I brought Duffy home and left him loose near the door between
the garage and the kitchen through which Connie always entered in
the evening. I squatted down and hid behind the wide counter that
divided the kitchen from the family room and waited. When she

entered, he ran to greet her and she exclaimed, *"Duffy*, what are you doing here?"

As for Gus—Gus thought that Duffy was the greatest dog toy since the invention of the tennis ball. The two guys jaw-wrestled for 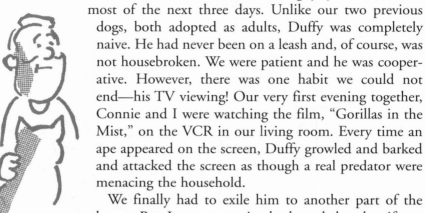most of the next three days. Unlike our two previous dogs, both adopted as adults, Duffy was completely naive. He had never been on a leash and, of course, was not housebroken. We were patient and he was cooperative. However, there was one habit we could not end—his TV viewing! Our very first evening together, Connie and I were watching the film, "Gorillas in the Mist," on the VCR in our living room. Every time an ape appeared on the screen, Duffy growled and barked and attacked the screen as though a real predator were menacing the household.

We finally had to exile him to another part of the house. But I was secure in the knowledge that if any savage animal ever emerged from the television set, Duffy would be our protector!

Duffy and Katie in Pacifica

In 1996 we moved from our ranch house in Foster City to a two-story cottage in Pacifica about a mile from the ocean. Although Pacifica is renown for its chilly mists, our new home was in a relatively fog-free area known as Vallemar. By then, the remarkable Gus had died. He could never be replaced but we had our obdurate but loveable Scottish Terrier, "Katie Scarlet."

Here we would learn new lessons about dog intelligence. (Remember, all this anthropomorphic, anthropocentric talk is to be viewed with suspicion!)

Pets are much more intelligent than we humans generally give them credit for. Duffy is a case in point. Not only does he watch television every evening, interacting with all the animals that appear, growling, barking, and chasing them, he also has memorized all the TV programs and commercials in which animals appear. At the first bar of the musical theme for such a program or commercial, Duffy goes on full alert, sitting on his haunches before the TV set, waiting for his prey.

A few years ago, my wife and I traveled to Europe to conduct research for my book on the sectarian group known as "Smith's Friends" and to visit my wife's relatives in Norway. We left our house and pets in the care of my mother-in-law, Betty, and her sister, Aggie.

On the first day after our departure, Aggie was alone in our living room, working on her needlepoint. At 4:30 P.M. Duffy took up a position at her feet, staring intently at her. Aggie did not know that Duffy had trained his humans to feed him promptly at 4:30, so she continued with her work.

Duffy cleared his throat. Aggie did not respond. Duffy yelped twice. Still no response. Duffy barked sharply. Aggie did briefly wonder if he were hungry, but assuming that his dinner hour was much later paid no attention. Duffy growled, barked, and pushed off with his paws against her thighs. Aggie was flustered but tried to ignore him. At this point, Duffy had had enough. He picked up her sewing basket in his jaws and carried it to the kitchen, depositing it near his food dish. Aggie got the point, and Duffy got his dinner.

Dog Intelligence?

Yes, it's true that pets are much more intelligent than we humans give them credit for—but not always. Take Katie for instance. When Gus died, we decided we wanted a second terrier to keep Duffy occupied so that he would stop eating the books on the lower shelves in my library. At the nearby SPCA we registered our preference for a terrier—a Westie, a Scottie, or a Cairn.

"It keeps returning to 'Animal Planet'!"

Shortly thereafter, when we returned from work one Friday night, there was a message on the answering machine asking us to come to the shelter. The next morning, we arrived before opening time and were just barely the first in line to see an abandoned, sun-bleached terrier that was desperately in need of a haircut. A woman from the local Scottish Terrier Rescue Society had brought a potential adopter who had equal claim to the dog. While our competitor thought it over, we immediately proceeded with the adoption—filling out the papers and paying the required fee. The Scottie rescuer tried to dissuade us by declaring, "These are not lap dogs, you know." We replied that we already had a Westie and were familiar with terrier eccentricities. (Duffy had always been a snugly lap dog, by the way, but I didn't let on.)

The dog's appearance told us that she had been kept outdoors for months on end and that she was neglected. Her owners had given her up because she repeatedly dug out from under their yard fence and escaped. The ID computer chip in her ear meant that someone had once treasured her. Something had gone wrong, however; perhaps her original owner had died.

The rescuer then offered to clip the dog. She had brought her grooming tools with her. Under the mass and tangle of unkempt fur, we found, to my great delight, a black Scottish Terrier—a breed I had always admired because they reminded me of FDR's "little dog Fala." She was scarcely the "Cocoa" her earlier owners had named her. This dog is so black that we cannot find her in our yard at night. The trick is to look for a spot that is blacker than all the other dark places and that's her!

Connie decided that the best way to insure that Katie would end her wandering ways would be to bond with her. For hours each day, Connie would hold the dog against her breast and reassure her. (To this day, whenever Connie sits or reclines on the living room furniture, Katie is in her lap!)

Scotties and Westies are small dogs that are unaware of their tiny size. In their minds, they are lions! Wherever we walked Katie, she would challenge, even threaten, larger dogs with her bear-trap-like jaw. We restrained her when she went after two Rhodesian Ridgebacks at our pet food store (which invites owners to bring their dogs into the shop with them). My grandsons were not as careful. Once when they were walking her, they let her get away from them and she bit a passer-by's Labrador on the shoulder.

Our Vallemar home was on a corner lot surrounded by a white picket fence. There was a great deal of foot traffic on both streets—adults, children, and dogs. Our neighbor Maggie was walking by one evening with her Doberman Pinscher, and the animal stuck his head through the pickets to sniff Katie. The bear trap snapped shut on his nose. The Doberman never made that mistake again. From a second-floor window, I used to watch with amusement as the huge dog wrestled and hauled his owner clear to the other side of the street whenever they walked past our house.

Katie Goes Underground

Katie has her own way of doing everything. When she walks, she drags her feet, producing a scraping sound like that of a geriatric patient shuffling along in house slippers. Her usual pace is about as speedy as a turtle.

On those rare occasions when she is overwhelmed by the sheer joy of life, she runs in a manner suggesting a fat man in an unbuttoned double-breasted suit chasing a taxicab! Her back legs dig in and propel her long body forward in a high arc. Her front legs touch the ground and her body catches up as though it were a stretched Slinky returning to its original compressed state. A soundtrack of *boing, boing, boing* should accompany her movements.

Katie is a digger. Her constant tunneling under fences was the reason given by her previous owner for placing her for adoption. She would dig her way to freedom and wander the neighborhood. Considering her appearance when we met her at the shelter, she must have spent all of her time out in the open. Her fur was sun bleached and probably had not been groomed for the greater part of her life.

Scottish Terriers, with their short, powerful legs and their bear-trap-like jaws were bred to hunt varmints such as moles and weasels, so it is not surprising that they dig. We were tolerant of her burrowing, filling in the holes in our yard as quickly as she excavated them, occasionally replacing a rosebush or other decorative plant that she destabilized. Then she underhandedly undertook the undermining of our gazebo.

As I mentioned, our home in Pacifica, "Rose Gate Cottage by the Sea," stood at the intersection of two streets. At the very corner of our lot was a huge, attractive, and practically useless gazebo. A gazebo is a freestanding roofed structure usually open on the sides. Ours stood fifteen feet high, was octagonal in shape, and was fully open on one side where it could be entered by climbing a three-step staircase. The other sides were lattice to about waist height and then open up to the roof, which was artistically domed and peaked and surmounted by a cast-iron weather vane. The floor was wood and sat on footings of solid concrete.

A gazebo is frequently designed to command a view. Ours presented pedestrians walking past our house, the banks of the creek that divided one of the streets, and century-old, towering eucalyptus and palm. Occasionally I would read my morning paper and drink a cup of coffee there. However, the constant comings and goings of chatty

"I found a stray kitty. Can I keep it?"

passersby, the rat-tat-tat of industrious woodpeckers, and the din of running school children made it a less-than-ideal retreat.

The only advantage of the structure was that it was a landmark. When I gave potential visitors driving directions, I would always tell them to turn left at the gazebo. One visitor, who came to our house to see a pool table that we were selling, played solo billiards on the table's green felt for several minutes, chatted interminably, and then nervously asked me, "Where do you keep your gazebo?" I pointed to it through the nearest window as he exclaimed, "Oh, that little house! I thought a gazebo was some kind of African animal and that you kept it tied up in the backyard." I suspect he thought a gazebo was a cross between a gazelle and a zebra!

Anyway, back to Katie. One day, she decided to tunnel under the "little house." She almost made it, but became stuck about three feet from a hole that was her intended exit. Connie discovered her and tried unsuccessfully to lure her closer so that we could grab her head and pull her out, but Katie just backed away with only her pink tongue visible in the darkness. After twenty minutes of pleading with Katie to come toward us, Connie, who is the most unflappable, calm person I know, became first frustrated, then alarmed, and, finally, to quote her self-appraisal, "nutsy." She said she was going to get a sledgehammer and break the floor. Then she proposed renting a crane

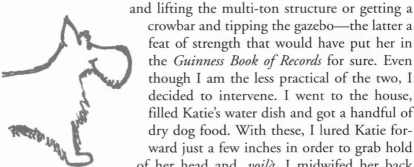 and lifting the multi-ton structure or getting a crowbar and tipping the gazebo—the latter a feat of strength that would have put her in the *Guinness Book of Records* for sure. Even though I am the less practical of the two, I decided to intervene. I went to the house, filled Katie's water dish and got a handful of dry dog food. With these, I lured Katie forward just a few inches in order to grab hold of her head and, *voilà*, I midwifed her back into the light of day.

Today, years later, Katie still loves to dig holes in the yard and if one of us leaves a gate or a door ajar, Katie will take off and wander the neighborhood until someone discovers her phone number on her collar or she finds her own way home. But never in the past several years has she tunneled again.

"Okay, what have you guys been up to?"

Hold Your Horses!

> . . . horses don't love people though the people may love their animals.
>
> Horses prefer to be the dominant ones with people and especially among themselves. Horses will try to gain dominance over their handlers—you can count on it.
>
> —Skip Crawford, horse trainer

Prior to the arrival of Stormy and Rags, I saw horses as extremely affectionate creatures. Certainly other people's horses always seemed to love me—to want to nuzzle my clothes, to offer their heads to be rubbed and patted. But not my horses!

Stormy—taller than my wife and substantial in all dimensions—simply does not like having her face touched. She is imperious. She bullies the smaller Rags shamelessly, chasing him from his food by running toward him with her ears pinned back or biting him in the rear. On rare occasions, he responds with a weak kick as he retreats, but mostly he gives way.

My wife's cousin Sherry, an experienced horsewoman, says that if Stormy were a person, she would be Tallulah Bankhead. And I suppose that if Rags were a person, he would be Don Knotts!

Horses are not pets. Or so I keep telling myself. But I do a poor job of convincing myself. I want them to be pets. At best, I must confess, horses are a strange crossbreed—half pet and half transportation vehicle.

During our first year together, Stormy would attempt to bite me whenever she could. She got me in the chest once (*ouch!*) and I dodged

"I can't whistle, so come running when you hear me play!"

her thereafter. One day, I was picking up windblown debris in our sand-ed arena while Stormy stood just over the fence in the pasture. As I walked toward the stable with a stray section of a two-by-four in my hand, she reached over the fence and lunged at me—a very foolish thing to do. Totally by reflex, I swatted her in the forehead with the piece of lumber. She has never bitten me since!

An early concern of mine was that I cannot whistle a note. How could I ever be a cowboy? How could I ever persuade a horse to come when summoned? What should I do? Should I shout, wave, send an e-mail? Could Roy himself have gotten Trigger's attention without a two-fingers-in-the-mouth whistle?

Well, I may not be able to whistle but I can sing. So I trained Stormy to respond to "Stormy Weather." I sing. Her ears tilt toward me and she approaches—when she feels like it. When we added Rags to our animal family, "Ragtime Cowboy Joe" worked.

About the time our neighbors began wondering about the impromptu concerts, I adopted a singsong "Stooowr-mee" and "Raah-aahgs," which became just as effective. Usually Rags starts toward me as soon as I call while Stormy stands still as a statue. When she sees him in motion, she figures that there may be something good in store for her so she overtakes him and he submissively makes way.

When we acquired Stormy and Rags, I was entering my sixties—about thirty years too old to start riding. My injuries to date:

1. A concussion from attempting to ride Stormy bareback. I jumped from a fence onto her back, went completely over her, and fell

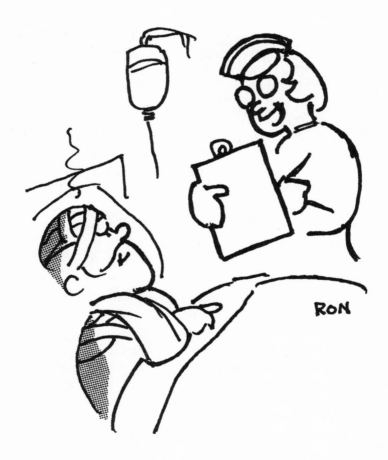

"And how is our little buckaroo this morning?"

on my head. The next thing I knew, I was sitting on our backyard deck, drinking a glass of lemonade. On the way to the emergency room, I kept asking Connie what had happened and she would tell me and a minute later I would ask all over again.

2. A broken collarbone. It was a Saturday morning. Connie was visiting her sister in Idaho and back in Shasta County we had a terrible firestorm that destroyed about a hundred homes only a few miles away. The smoke-filled wind was blowing in gusts of up to fifty miles an hour. I went out to offer Stormy her morning meal, and then placed two flakes of hay in the wallhung manger in her stall and was walking away to check the water tank. From over my shoulder, I heard the pounding of galloping hooves and turned toward the sound just as Stormy's massive head connected with my right clavicle, throwing me through the air like the proverbial rag doll. Stormy ran twenty yards, stopped, and turned toward me, looking confused and befuddled. I returned to the house, phoned my wife's Aunt Aggie, who, in turn, summoned her son-in-law Don to get me to a medical clinic.

When I arrived back home, I discovered that Katie had rousted a skunk from under the deck with the usual skunk versus dog results. My potential helpers were occupied saving horses from the firestorm and could not help me. So with my right arm out of action, I dragged Katie into the bathtub and washed her with the special skunk deodorizing shampoo we keep on hand. (It is a real chore for me to lift Katie under normal circumstances. Though she weighs only twenty-eight pounds, she has the ability to tense her muscles in such a way that all of her bulk seems to shift to whatever place I am not supporting. Suddenly, she feels like a hundred-pound sandbag!)

3. A second concussion. Just before we bought Rags, Connie gave me as a birthday present an eight-lesson course in riding at a local equine academy. Lessons seven and eight had been postponed due to a scheduling conflict. In the meantime, Rags had entered the picture. So I proposed that in lieu of the two lessons, I pick up the instructor and bring him to our place for a lesson, and then return him to the school. That way I could take my session on my own horse instead of the academy's lesson horse.

The instructor had me mount Rags in our sanded arena and ride him into our fifty-foot round pen. Totally focused on keeping my balance, I did not look ahead, and ran right into the archway at the entrance to the pen, which threw me backwards to the ground. In true cowboy tradition, the instructor urged me to remount, which I did. I was riding Rags at a walk when he suddenly sped up, making me feel as if I were about to fall off. Keeping the reins in one hand, I grabbed the saddle horn with the other—just as an old wrangler we know had told me to do if I were ever in this predicament. The instructor shouted repeatedly for me to let go. When I finally did, I fell, landing

"Katie, anything you do from now on will be an improvement!"

"Go ahead, refuse to 'whoa' now!"

between the horse and the crossbars of the fence. I was knocked unconscious. Fortunately, I was wearing a riding helmet and a flack jacket. When I awoke, the bill of the helmet was down over my chin.

After a long hiatus to regain the use of my entire body as well as to recover my confidence—and with the help of a new and more cautious riding instructor—I tried again. Even though I have only lately graduated to riding outside of our fifty-foot round pen, Rags and I are making great progress in the sanded arena. A folk song refrain describes "horses that have never been rode and cowboys who have never been throwed." Well, for better or worse, Rags and I belong to neither category!

RON

"No offense Rev., but maybe you should stick to saving souls!"

Stormy's ride is as smooth and comfortable as she is big and beautiful. In addition, she is amazingly calm. She stands still for haltering, grooming, hoof picking, saddling, bitting, etc. But don't try to put insect repellent lotion on her face. She will respond by cocking a rear leg at you or turning her rump toward you or stalking away.

Rags is more of a jitterbug—dancing around while I try to groom him, bending his head and neck toward me when I am picking his hooves so that he can nibble on my rump. Once he is saddled, he is a perfect gentleman, eager to give his rider whatever is asked of him.

And that "speed up" problem (still memorialized by a pronounced bend in the bars of the round pen where my helmet struck metal), that's under control. If he increases his speed without a command from me, a gentle tugging on the reins slows him to a pace that is comfortable for me.

Stormy and Rags Go to College

Connie always wanted a horse. Her greatest regret is that she waited until she was almost sixty before obtaining Stormy. I was sixty-one when we bought Rags. When it came to horses, we were as green as grass. We were "newbies," full of aspirations and anxieties.

Stormy had belonged to a local woman and her daughters and was used to being ridden. When Rags was brought to our area, two weeks before we bought him, he was so thin that he was nicknamed "Scarecrow." In addition, he was so faded in color that his red roan hues were scarcely visible. Rags had been a Hollywood ranch horse. A year of regular, improved diet and personal care gave him beautiful form and color. He had a puppy-dog-like trait of following me as close as my shadow, showing affection and mooching for treats.

As neophytes, we sought all the guidance we could find—from experienced horse owners, equine events, feed stores, books, magazines, and television shows on RFD-TV. We had a year of lessons on our own property to build up our confidence and were ready to trailer the horses and involve them in activities with other horses and riders. Then we thought of Shasta College, which offers equine courses in their "Ag" department. (Remember—we live in the country!)

Today our two horses have the distinction of being college educated. In 2001, Connie signed up for courses in Western and English riding at our local community college, which is about twenty miles from our home. When the first course began, I helped Connie load Stormy into our trailer and off we went, leaving a very frantic Rags at home. As we discovered, horses are very herd bound. Ours whinny and shriek at the top of their lungs when separated, setting up a pathetic racket, soon joined in their complaints by "the old gentlemen," our neighbor's retired thoroughbreds.

For the first few weeks, I accompanied Connie to class, helping load the large mare at home, unload her at school, tack her up before class, untack her after class, reload her for the homeward journey, and, finally, unload her as she and Rags squealed with delight. At class we met Dawn, a young student who lived near us in Cottonwood. Dawn was horseless. She had sold her horse just after the semester began, so we arranged a swap of services: we would bring Rags for Dawn to ride if she would take over my duties, including loading the horses at our ranch. Occasionally I still attended class as a spectator.

In the beginning, it was not difficult to load Rags. But one incident changed that. As Connie wrote in her journal:

> When we got to the campus, I was about to release the lead rope that connects Rags' halter to the front of the trailer so that I could unload him, when suddenly Ag students appeared, headed to another part of the campus and driving PIGS! Now, pigs unnerve horses. Rags pulled back on his tie, tried to rear, and, in the process, banged his head on the ceiling of the trailer. I quickly closed the side windows to wait for the pigs to pass. Rags became agitated and fidgety, sweating heavily.
>
> Things didn't get any better. Dawn rode Stormy today. Laurel, another experienced student, rode Rags to warm him up for me. When she took off her baseball cap, Rags was spooked. He bolted and Laurel fell off. Rags kept on going, running in circles.
>
> Laurel was embarrassed but otherwise OK.

From this point on, loading Rags would, with few exceptions, prove to be a frustrating chore.

At class, Connie decided to switch from Stormy to Rags now and then, just to gain confidence in riding both horses. One day as Connie was on Rags, he began fussing with his feet, which caused his running martingale, a training device used for steadying a horse's head, to slip down his neck, settling around his ears. All of a sudden, he panicked, bucked, and reared, throwing Connie into the air. I watched in horror, unable to do anything but wait for her return to earth. Her hang time was outstanding! She landed on her hip and back with an appalling thud. Rags reared again, "Hi, yo, Silver!" style, flipped completely over, and landed on his back. In true cowboy spirit, Connie remounted Rags and continued with the lesson.

On another occasion, Rags was well behaved but Stormy was not. Connie recalls:

> Today we are taking both horses to class. Dawn wants to work with Rags. She came over on the weekend to ride him and practice loading him. He remembered his last lesson and was not bad at all about loading. He was also quiet while she rode him. He seems to be confused about slowing from a lope to a jog or walk.
>
> At Class, I saw a side of Stormy I've never seen before, calling to Rags and reacting with alarm at being separated from him when he was even a few yards away from her. She was very inattentive. I had a lot of trouble getting her to stop on command or otherwise respond to me. Her attitude for the day could be summed up as "You're not the boss of me!"

Today Was Not Fun!

A horse can be perfectly well behaved on his home turf but take him to a class at a new place with strange sights, scenes, and odors, mix him with other horses and riders and his calm, cooperative frame of mind can evaporate. Horses have moods—just as people do. And the sooner novice riders recognize that this is so, the better able they will be to manage and guide their mounts and to ride safely. Like all animals, individual horses have individual personalities. Rags is eager to please; Stormy is not. Rags is respectful—he lifts his head from his morning hay and stands at attention when I slip his fly mask over his ears and eyes. Stormy defiantly pins her ears back and keeps her head down in her food as if to say, "Get lost, Puny Biped. *I'm eating here!*"

In contrast, after Stormy has finished feeding and is loafing near the barn, she becomes docile and allows us to trim her face and feet with a buzzing electric clippers without so much as our having to put a halter or lead rope on her.

Stormy is usually calm and steady. When I first mounted her and fell off, she did not move a muscle. Rags is on the timid side and is easily startled. In nature, horses are prey. They rely on quick reflexes and speed to escape danger. A plastic bag blowing in the wind or a paper towel in the hands of one of his owners can cause Rags to rear or run away.

But not every riding class was characterized by frustration, unwanted adventure, and anxiety. "Some days," Connie observes, "I really had the feeling of horse and rider being one. At times, we were both on the same wavelength. Stormy was responsive to all my commands. As I became a confident rider, her actions mirrored my sense of assurance. All I could do at the end of such rides was say, 'Thank you.' At times like these, the hard work seemed to find its reward. These were the moments I had been dreaming of!"

The training Connie did in the classes prepared horse and rider for maneuvers such as side passing, jogging or loping in patterns around obstacles, stopping, and spinning. She learned how to give the horse "cues" with her hands, legs, voice, and body movements.

As part of the Western class final exam, Connie and Rags performed a trail course and a reining pattern. Connie states, "The patterns weren't perfect but I was proud of finishing and all that we had accomplished."

Earlier I mentioned that as a birthday present, Connie had given me eight lessons at a local riding school. After my two falls, I was an overcautious rider. Time and lessons with a new, more careful instructor brought Rags and me to a sense of partnership and security, even though I never ride without wearing a foam-lined helmet and a padded safety vest. After all, thanks to modern protective gear, there's never been a safer time to ride—or fall off—a horse.

Some of the greatest rewards of horse ownership have come from sharing our "country life-style" with our grandchildren. Connie remarks:

> Our oldest grandson, Jonathan, was with us when we purchased Stormy, Jake came with me for a week's worth of riding lessons, and both boys learned alongside us the care and feeding of our horses. At first it was my duty to saddle two horses, sometimes twice a day for them to ride. Now Jonathan is in charge of tacking them up. He assists Jessica, his young sister, into the saddle and leads her in our round pen. He and Jake ride with assurance. I sure wish I had started in my teens!

And so it goes.

Rags Meets the "Horse Whisperer"

Monty Roberts, internationally renowned "horse whisperer," was coming to town. The horse community was ecstatic. The local newspaper reported that Monty was recruiting "problem horses" (or "horses with people problems," to be more exact) for the demonstrations he would be conducting. Although we and our friends had tried everything short of lethal force, our beloved Rags could not be cajoled into entering a horse trailer. At times it took us up to three hours to get him aboard. A fit challenge for Monty Roberts, I reckoned. (Own a horse long enough and one begins to sound like a cowboy.)

I phoned the arena where Monty would be appearing and was told the auditions were being held at noon the day of the event.

Connie, Mary Lou (an extremely experienced horseperson we knew), and I started loading Rags in the early morning. Finally, we succeeded and drove to the arena. About a dozen horses were being considered for the four starring roles in the evening performance. Among them were some of the wildest, stubbornest, rankest cayuses imaginable. As Monty watched from a distance, each owner and Monty's assistants paraded the animals, one at a time, for inspection. Their problems were vividly demonstrated and keenly examined. Sweet, cute Rags was his reprobate best and won the feature spot at the conclusion of the demonstration schedule. I was so proud that I was to have the worst horse in the show!

That evening, after Monty worked his magic with three horses—for instance, taming a previously unbroken mustang in minutes and riding a high-strung Friesian for the first time—Rags entered the center ring. After he and Monty befriended one another by joining up and Rags circled the ring a few times, Monty applied his custom designed halter to Rags and led him to a posh horse trailer about the size of a navy destroyer.

Without hesitation, Rags followed Monty into the vehicle. Then Monty called Connie into the act and had her guide Rags into the trailer. A beautiful performance by horse and humans, which was

"I *was* showing her who's boss!"

accompanied by gasps of wonderment and followed by thunderous applause!

Then it was time to trailer Rags for the homeward journey in our scant two-horse, side-by-side rig. No go! Rags refused. Monty was nowhere to be seen. This time, it took the three of us only twenty minutes to get Rags into his limousine. And that remains about the average.

Are Horses Expensive?

I am often asked this, usually in the form of a rhetorical question, the inquirer assuming that the answer is "yes."

Our horses cost $2,000 each—but that was only the beginning. Some would say, "the beginning of the end" as detailed in a widely distributed anecdote:

A friend gives you a horse . . .
You build a small shelter . . . $750
You fence in a paddock . . . $450
Purchase small truck to haul hay . . . $12,000
Purchase a two-horse trailer . . . $2,800
Purchase second horse . . . $2,500
Build larger shelter with storage . . . $2,000
More fencing . . . $3,200
Purchase third horse . . . $3,000
Purchase four-horse trailer . . . $7,500
Purchase larger truck . . . $24,000
Purchase four acres next door . . . $28,000
More fencing . . . $4,000
Build small barn . . . $16,000
Purchase camper for truck . . . $9,000
Purchase tractor . . . $12,000
Purchase fourth and fifth horses . . . $6,500
Purchase twenty acres . . . $185,000
Build house . . . $135,000
Build barn . . . $36,000
More fencing and corrals . . . $24,000
Build covered arena . . . $82,000
Purchase more powerful truck . . . $34,000
Purchase gooseneck trailer with living quarters . . . $32,000

Purchase sixth, seventh and eighth horses . . . $10,750
Hire full-time trainer . . . $40,000 per annum
Build house for trainer . . . $84,000
Buy motor home for shows . . . $125,000
Purchase fancy, silver-studded saddle, tack, clothes, boots, and hat for shows . . . $12,000
Hire attorney. Wife leaving you for trainer...$5,000
Declare bankruptcy; wife gets everything.
Friend feels sorry for you . . . gives you a horse . . . .

Are Horses Stupid?

My son Stephen, whom I consider "the world's leading authority" on almost everything, insists that horses are stupid. His opinion is based on his experiences as a hot-air-balloon pilot.

As a balloonist, Steve can always decide from where to ascend. Where to descend is another matter. Steve prefers farmers' fields and ranchers' pastures. While he is busy bringing the balloon back to earth, his "chase crew" on the ground monitors him by eye and by two-way radio. Often such farm animals as cows and horses occupy his selected landing site.

Steve notes that the horses have a nasty habit of taking flight and, in their panic, running straight into farm fences! Such injury to livestock does not endear balloonists to the animals' owners.

Looking at the matter from my perspective as an equine rancher, I have to ask, "Who is really stupid? The intrepid aviator who allows himself to have no choice but to land when and where the wind carries him? Or the frightened animals?"

Admittedly, horses have very small brains—about the size of an adult human's thumb—but they are canny and adaptable.

Stormy can undo gate latches as well as chains secured with spring clasps with the skill of Houdini! Once, when I tried to restrict her to one of our two pastures by closing and securing the gate between them, she stood on her side of the gate, eye to eye with me, removed the clasp with her prehensile lips and tongue, and spat it at my feet.

Another time, I made the mistake of leaving a fifty-pound bag of feed out in the open several feet from her paddock area. Once again, I believed that a gate secured with a chain and clasp would suffice. The next morning I found the gate ajar, the bag split open, and one-third of its contents gone!

Rags is more subtle. If we take our eyes off him for a minute, he will creep away from his morning hay and try to silently tiptoe into his stall to eat his evening meal. My sprinting speed has increased noticeably since he joined us!

Purr the Empress, "Leapin' Lizard!"

Women and cats will do as they please, and men and dogs should relax and get used to the idea.
—Robert A. Heinlein

We ordered our Himalayan kitten from a pet store, which had her flown in from Washington State. At the time, we lived in Pacifica near the ocean. To keep her safe from the dogs, we dedicated a spare bedroom to her, naming it "Kitty City" and furnishing it with cat toys, a scratching post, a cat bed, a litter box, and food and water dishes. If Katie or Duffy bothered her, she would hide behind the furniture in this room. The room was on the second floor and I usually read and watched TV on the first, calling her to me by imitating a cat's meow. Since I worked at home while Connie was away for the day at work, Purr and I bonded. In Connie's words, "You stole my cat!"

When we moved to Cottonwood and added Nehi to our menagerie, Purr was less than a year old. Nehi, then a puppy not much larger than Purr, loved to chase Purr and would try to stop her by placing a paw on her head. This upset Connie, who thought that Purr would be harmed. My take on the situation was different: I thought they were playing. One evening, Sandy, Connie's cousin's daughter, a California Highway Patrol officer and an expert when it comes to equines and felines, was visiting us. Sandy is single and there are always at least three cats sharing her home. We were relaxing after dinner, swapping favorite pet stories, when suddenly Purr ran across Sandy's lap, followed by the ardent Nehi. Connie expressed her fears and I countered with my theory, when all at once the animals reversed direction and the cat pursued the dog, round and round the sofa, over Sandy's lap!

Often they would sleep together on the same dog bed.

Most of the time, the dogs and Purr ignore one another, Purr walking over them or pushing her way through their midst to get to her food. Sometimes one or more of the dogs decides it would be fun to chase her and she obliges by running away—if she is in the mood. While Purr is outracing them, short-legged Katie loves to bellow her ferocious bark just to prove that she really is a dog! Two short steps and Katie gives up the chase. On other occasions, Purr simply joins the pack—napping in the dogs' beds and among their playthings, fearlessly sampling their food, seemingly indifferent to their presence!

I have mentioned that Purr adopted me. Once or twice a day, she summons me with her imperial meow to groom her. Sometimes she pays me for my services with a freshly killed bird! (Unlike Tassy, she does not eat her prey.)

Since Purr is a very small cat in a very large fur coat, grooming her requires Jobian patience, mutual tolerance, and considerable skill. Her forays through our hay room, bushes, grass, and shrubs contribute all sorts of thorns, burrs, branches, and other debris—all of which become firmly woven into her coat. And even without the foreign matter, her long, dense hair plaits itself into every manner of knot and snarl. A grooming session consists of three parts:

> Purr approaches, usually when I am at the computer, and demands attention. She jumps into my lap or, depending on her mood, waits impatiently for me to lift her.

I brush her head, behind her ears in particular, and she purrs in appreciation. I brush her back and sides as the purring continues.

Then comes the ordeal. I attempt to detangle, deknot, and delete the plant and field matter from her fur. I pluck. I brush. I curry. I cut. And Purr? She struggles, whines, snarls, hisses, and claws me as she attempts to wrestle her way out of my grip.

Her sounds of distress often bring the dogs, which in sympathy nuzzle her, only causing more resistance. Recently, as I was cutting a snarl from her hip, the twisting and pulling took my attention away from the scissors I was closing and I cut a chunk of flesh out of my beloved cat.

I have never felt guiltier in my life and, for weeks, Purr was my friend no longer. She even went so far as to spend one evening in Connie's lap! Purring! Imagine that! Fortunately, most of the time, pets are magnanimous and our previous congenial relationship has returned—almost. She will come over to me and sit in my lap for up to twenty minutes at a time while I stroke her and scratch her throat and behind her ears. But as of yet without purring!

Today there was a definite breakthrough. It is 105° and the hot winds have dried out the weeds, leaving burrs, chaff, and stickers—all of which are attracted to her fur like iron filings to a magnet. She came to me twice to be groomed and purred during one visit. Then she went out into the backyard and brought me a lovely seven-inch-long lizard—alive! She released it and it is now residing under the sofa where I was sitting. (I hope it enjoys living here with all the other animals.)

But whether or not Purr decides to forgive me, from now on, I think I will leave the cat detangling to the professionals. I find dogs and horses to be much more forgiving than cats!

P. S. I learned a better grooming technique from fellow Himmie owner Martha Stewart. She *combs*—not brushes—her Himalayan cats daily. I have abandoned the curry brush and both Purr and I are happier!

Rizzi the Charismatic

I've seen a look in dogs' eyes, a quickly vanishing look of amazed contempt, and I am convinced that basically dogs think humans are nuts.

—John Steinbeck

In the summer of 2002, wildfires rampaged through the Western states from California to Oklahoma. Especially devastated was Carizzo, an Apache Indian reservation in Arizona. Countless homes and other buildings were lost and millions of dollars of tribally owned timber went up in smoke, causing the loss of hundreds of jobs.

Firefighters were called in from many places, near and far, including from the part of northern California where I live, which is a long two- or three-day drive from the scene of the blaze.

As our local fire team battled the blaze, a small, very pregnant dog adopted the crew. When the fire was under control, they searched for the dog's owners but the Native Americans who lived there had no idea where she had come from or to whom she belonged. So the firefighters took her along with them. She had won them over with her constant attention, affection, and playfulness. She also was fiercely protective of the men and women of the crew, chasing away other animals that approached the firefighters' ever-wandering campsites. They named her "Carizzo" after the fire and brought her back to California.

Carizzo

She had a litter of puppies so cute that they were quickly adopted. The little mother took up residence with one member of the crew, who found that he could not keep her in his condo. He passed her on to another crewmember, a young woman who had adopted one of the puppies. This crewmember placed the little dog for adoption with a feed store in our local area. This particular store has a few wire cages between their two front entrances where they display dogs and cats available for adoption at no cost.

Connie and I spotted her in her cage as we pulled into the store's parking area. Because she was about half the size of Nehi, our Queensland Heeler/McNab cross, I incorrectly assumed that she was a puppy. The store clerk informed me that she was a full-grown dog that had just borne a litter. In body type and general coloration, she resembled a tiny Nehi, but she was tricolor—black, white, and amber—and her face was very different. She had a raccoonlike mask, amber and black with amber spots above both eyes like pseudo-eyes. It was as though a fox terrier face had been grafted on a dog like Nehi.

"But I *did* ask you first, and
you said that's all we needed around here!"

A few days earlier, our wonderful Duffy had died just short of his fourteenth birthday and Connie had repeatedly insisted that the two remaining dogs, Katie and Nehi, were more than enough. But as Connie and Carizzo stared at one another through the mesh of the cage—well, let's let Connie tell the story:

> It was love at first sight! It happened the instant she gazed at me with soft brown eyes, promising love, comfort, and lasting joy. There was no hesitation, no question of our compatibility.
>
> I was older; she had a mysterious past—it was of no consequence. Any differences would work out over time.
>
> She smiled her funny little self-conscious, toothy grin and leaned into me for the reassurance from me that she had found the one she had been searching for.
>
> We both knew it. We would be together forever.

Connie had removed the little dog from the cage, and been rewarded with a blizzard of wet kisses, while I engaged the clerk in a short conversation that led to "Rizzi" (short for "Carizzo") becoming an official member of the Streiker family (also known as "what a zoo!").

She has been with us now for about five months and no dog has won such general acceptance so immediately from us, from our dogs, our surviving cat, our neighbors, their dogs, visitors, relatives, and passersby. She is simply magnetic; one could say charismatic. Part of her charm is the fact that when approached, she smiles. How can anyone not love a dog who smiles at him?

"This isn't going to work if you don't stop smiling at everybody!"

"Is everyone comfy?"

She is also a handful. She is almost as intelligent as Nehi, which is saying a lot, but even more athletic. The four-foot-high farm fences on our property are no obstacles to her. She either clears them in a single bound or scrambles a bit to the top in order to jump over. At night, when we put the animals in the kitchen and seal it off with a baby gate, she clears that gate in a graceful leap! I even tried placing a second baby gate above the first but she simply hurdled the counter that separates the kitchen from the rest of the house. So she sleeps with us, between us in our bed. (I am grateful that neither of the horses has been this insistent.)

She is a natural shepherd of large animals. "It's in her blood," my country neighbors frequently tell me. Since the only large animals we

Inevitably, the ability to shepherd large
animals had a downside.

have are the two horses, Rizzi takes as her daily responsibility the job of gathering them and heading them for our stable so that they can be put up for the night. Perhaps "heading" misstates the matter. She is in fact a Queensland Blue Heeler, a breed that was recently officially renamed "Australian Cattle Dog." Indeed, she is a "heeler." She barks and nips at the heels of the horses until they are moving in the right direction.

When I leave the house in the early evening on the way to the stable, Rizzi takes up a position just outside the fence separating the sanded arena from the two pastures. As I walk from the house, she runs through the farthest gate into the pastures and directs the horses toward their evening food and accommodations. Stormy, our imperious mare, walks slowly and calmly toward the gate between the pastures and the paddock area outside her stall, apparently ignoring the tiny shepherd. She waits, slowly pawing the ground, as I remove her fly mask and let her into her paddock area so that she can get to her stall and to her dinner.

Rags has a different attitude, one that shouts, "You're not the boss of me!" He often turns his head toward her and tries to chase her away but she soon is at his heels and has him turned around. Rags kicks at her, first with one rear hoof and then with both at once, mule style. Rizzi is too close to the ground for Rags to connect—thank goodness! Soon he is exactly where Rizzi wants him to be, racing into his paddock area and stall as fast as he can move. I have to go into his stall to remove his mask. I dare not get in his path.

Her job done, Rizzi then accompanies me to the house. Sometimes when she is chasing the horses, Rizzi will leap into the air and grab hold of a horse's tail, swinging wildly through the air. When she is not rounding up horses, she concentrates on Connie's footwear. Connie's diminutive shoes and socks disappear from their proper places and end up in Rizzi's mouth. She shakes them violently, throws them a few feet, and then retrieves them, repeating the process a few times, occasionally dragging them into the backyard.

When given the "down" command, she rolls over on one side and extends the opposite leg into the air, expecting to have her tummy rubbed. She is absolutely promiscuous in offering that tummy to anyone who will interact with her. Whenever I wake in the morning, be it momentarily at 3:30 or fully at 7:30, she becomes aware of my state and licks my neck, ears, and face until I respond. Then she

"You say your watch dog smiled at the burgler, then got a tummy-rub from him. Did she help load the loot too?"

snuggles her back against me, lifts a leg straight up, and demands her belly rub.

The vet estimates that she is three years old. We had Nehi spayed when she was under a year old and she remained cheerful and loving during her recuperation. But Rizzi was a dog of another color! She was angry with us and withdrawn for about two weeks. No one can withhold affection like an offended Queensland!

Rizzi and Nehi, our "Aussie girls," are soul mates. In the house, they will suddenly wrestle ferociously for about ten minutes, Katie the disciplinarian barking at them all the while. In the backyard or the sanded arena, they will run full tilt in a chaotic race, first the taller, longer-legged Nehi in the lead, then Rizzi overtaking her with her graceful, flying strides. They become tangled together for an instant and then Nehi once again races ahead. Watching them walk or run side by side has an exhilarating effect on Connie and me. They are so affectionate and comfortable with one another and they just seem so suited. They are as lucky to have one another as we are to have them!

"I climbed it because it was there!"

Rizzi Goes to School

Don't accept your dog's admiration as conclusive evidence
that you are wonderful.

—Anonymous

When a man's best friend is his dog, that dog has a problem.
—Edward Abbey

Tomorrow night, we begin a new dog obedience class. This time
Rizzi is the student. Now, Rizzi is a wonderful, loving, fun-loving,
entertaining companion, but she is definitely rough around the edges.
She barks at the horses too much. She comes and goes as she pleases.
She does not always return when called. And although there is not a
more affectionate pet, she really overdoes it. I hope to learn some sim-
ple way to get her off my body and out of my face when I am not
eager to be smothered with dog kisses.

Further, I am concerned about her love of automobile and truck
rides. If I put her in the backyard and attempt to get into our Honda
sedan or our old Ford truck, she hurdles the fences and is in the pas-
senger seat of the car or truck before I can enter. (Well, at least she
doesn't honk the horn!)

I have to admit she is excellent company on the
road since she has overcome her tendency to
become carsick. The problem is that she will go
through any open vehicle door—whether it
belongs to a UPS truck, a neighbor's pickup, a
visitor's car, a police cruiser, or a fire engine.

I don't want to repress her *joie de vivre*.
Neighborhood children come to the door and ask
to see "the smiling dog. The nice one." I want her to
stay smiling and nice. I just want a bit more control
over her unruly exuberance—and her hitchhiking! I acknowledge that
some traits are unchangeable. Gus never learned to resist pumpkin

Watching humans carefully,
Rizzi learns early the art of sucking-up.

pies or female dogs. Cuddles always snapped at loud, nervous men. Nehi, the closest thing yet to a perfect dog, still barks ferociously with the hair on her neck standing upright when anyone comes to the door—be it friend, relative, next-door neighbor, or Connie in a Halloween costume. Realizing that there are limits to what a trainer may achieve, I press on, full of hope. (It took me a long time to complete this paragraph. Rizzi had jumped into my lap and was licking my face!)

Rizzi the Gourmet

We call Katie "the stealth dog" because she is invisible when in the yard at night. Rizzi evinces considerable furtiveness of her own, especially when it comes to MY FOOD! My son Stephen sends us a lovely box of frozen filet mignons every year as a Christmas present. We love to grill them on our George Foreman and serve them with baked potatoes. One night, Connie prepared the last two steaks, placed each of them on a plate with a potato, and called me to the dinner table. When I got there, my steak was missing. In five seconds, Rizzi had not only removed it but also consumed it!

When I called attention to my steak-empty plate, Connie assumed that I was playing a game. After all, she had only taken her eye off the table for a few seconds. At another mealtime, I made the mistake of leaving a slice of pizza while I left the room for a few minutes. Again, only an empty plate remained!

I guess I have been observing the first of "The Canine Ten Commandments":

1. Thou shalt not hide the food but shalt leave it in plain view.
2. Thou shalt feed me today more than thou didst yesterday.
3. Thou shalt teach me with food—not big sticks and loud voices.
4. Thou shalt walk with me every day—despite thy favorite TV program.
5. Thou shalt not buy furniture on which I cannot climb and sit.
6. Thou shalt not pay attention to anyone else but me—lest I feel unwanted.
7. Thou shalt love me to death—even when I bark all night.
8. Thou shalt not have a cat with ATTITUDE and CLAWS.

9. Thou shalt not start the car until I am in it.
10. Thou shalt obey the above without question and forgive me my trespasses both in thy living room and on thy neighbor's lawn.

"They're all spoiled. They demand motels with home atmosphere and a home with hotel service!"

Fetch!

Playing fetch with one of our dogs remains my all time favorite pet-human activity. I have already mentioned how, once Gus entered the picture, Cuddles showed herself to be a quick study when it came to the art of tennis ball retrieval. Gus himself needed no instruction. His legs being longer than hers, he would beat her to the target and return with the ball before she had traveled more than a few feet. From time to time, I would hold him by the collar to give her a head start. This worked for a while but soon she realized that she was outclassed and would not even try to retrieve.

The pattern repeated with Gus and Duffy. The younger, nimbler Duffy out-scrambled Gus and almost at once, Gus gave up the game.

When Nehi entered the competition, it was a replay of the earlier situations. Duffy retired as undefeated tennis ball hustler and Nehi took up the job. But here we faced a problem. Overenthusiastic Nehi not only overtook all objects thrown; she annihilated them. Tennis balls, baseballs, and softballs were her first victims. She tore them to pieces. So I substituted volleyballs, beach balls, and basketballs. If the ball had a cover, she would gnaw a carrying handle into its hide to make it easier for her to lug it. Finally, she would chew away at the cover until the ball was destroyed. Multicolored children's bouncing balls were instantly obliterated like so many balloons being popped.

Soccer balls were a specialty of hers. She would scoot them along the ground for several minutes at a time, looking as though she were trying out for the lead role in a Disney film about "the dog who played professional football in Australia." But eventually she skinned the soccer balls too.

If I did not instantly throw out the first ball of the day when I arose in the morning, Nehi would begin her persistent "woo-woo" bark, a combination of a hyena's howl, a beagle's baying, and the wail of a frail that was made part of the blues. Then Jolly Ball came to the rescue. The Jolly Ball is tough, rubbery ball about the size of a basketball. We had purchased two of them for our horses to amuse themselves with in hopes that they would stop playing with the auto tires that surround the pasture sprinklers. The horses love to drag the tires away and toss them into the air. Next they pull out the sprinkler heads.

I threw one of the balls into a pasture and hung the other on a rope between the horses' paddocks. The horses sniffed at the one on the ground once or twice and proceeded to ignore it in favor of the tires. The one between their paddocks never even attracted that much attention, so I decided to offer it to Nehi.

This turned out to be her favorite fetch toy ever! Not only is it vivaciously bouncy and, so far, remarkably indestructible but also there is a ring molded into it, which provides Nehi with the perfect handle when she decides that she has chased the ball enough and wants to bring it back to Connie or me for another toss.

We also keep a half-deflated volleyball on hand to relieve Jolly Ball boredom. Nehi can't seem to damage this and she is able to catch it in midair when we throw it in a high arc. The Jolly Ball is just too heavy and hard for flyball training.

So far Rizzi prefers to retrieve living targets such as the horses or our neighbor's three goats. However, when Nehi is not looking, Rizzi will go over to the Jolly Ball and lift it by its ring and move it a few feet just to show that she can.

In addition to collecting Connie's socks, shoes, slippers, and panty-hose, Rizzi also brings home all manner of baseballs, pet toys, children's toys, bunny slippers, and other collectibles from places unknown. I expect to have a county detective or an animal control officer at the door any day now! Since Rizzi can climb or hurdle virtually any fence, I sometimes fantasize about obtaining a ball and chain. Connie suggests we simply try taller fences.

"Rizzi has started eating solid foods now.
My socks, my shoes, my slippers . . . !"

"Here, Barky, Barky!"

Regarding barking, not only does each dog have his day but also his own distinctive woof. I find Katie's the most offensive, reminding me of a cannon being fired in a vacant warehouse or a cherry bomb exploding in an empty oil barrel. Katie's bark is enough to elicit posttraumatic stress syndrome in any war veteran! Katie barks when she wants to get back into the house, when she considers the playful combat of Nehi and Rizzi too exuberant, when she expects me to lift her onto the sofa where I am relaxing while watching TV, etc. Her most enthusiastic bark is reserved for whenever she exits the back door for the yard and she signals the neighborhood, "Beware! Katie has left the building!"

It is not the case with Katie that her bark is worse than her bite. All Scotties are feisty—I have watched with glee as President Bush futilely attempts to summon his Scottie, Barney. And, of course, I remember FDR's references to his spirited little dog, Fala:

> These Republican leaders have not been content with attacks on me, or my wife, or on my sons. No, not content with that, they now include my little dog, Fala. Well, of course, I don't resent attacks, and my family doesn't resent attacks, but Fala does resent them. You know, Fala is Scotch, and being a Scottie, as soon as he learned that the Republican fiction writers in Congress had gone out and had concocted a story that I had left him behind on the Aleutian Islands and had sent a destroyer back to find him—at a cost to the taxpayers of two or three, or eight or twenty million dollars—his Scotch soul was furious. He has not been the same dog since. I am accustomed to hearing malicious falsehoods about myself—such as that old, worm-eaten chestnut that I have represented myself as indispensable. But I think I have a right to resent, to object to libelous statements about my dog.
>
> —Sept. 23, 1944, address to the Teamsters Union

"... well it certainly wasn't *my* dog keeping her awake. Let me call him for you. Here, Barky. Here, Barky!"

In Katie's earlier days, she was downright aggressive with other dogs regardless of their size. The first night of her once-a-week obedience training class at the SPCA in Burlingame, she barked at and lunged after each of the other fifteen dogs in the class. She was so uncontrollable that I was asked to remove her from the scene. A week later, the instructor fitted her with a special pinch collar and Katie finally stopped struggling to get at her canine companions. Things went well for several weeks until the very final class—the graduation. A woman who had been in a class on another evening found that due to scheduling problem she would not be able to attend her final class so she was permitted to participate in ours. Katie had come to accept all her classmates but she was infuriated by the presence of this stranger and reverted to her previous attack mode—barking, snarling, and lunging at this strange dog.

I have mentioned how she tried to assail a pair of Rhodesian Ridgebacks—huge dogs that are used in Africa to hunt lions.

She was never hostile with our other dogs. In fact, at mealtime it was difficult to get her to eat from her dish while they ate from theirs. She shyly keeps her distance. When we moved from our suburban home to the country, her aggressiveness abated. Neighbors' dogs and cats frequently visit the property, some jumping the backyard fences to stop over. Katie ignores them.

Cuddles was suspicious of human males other than me. When any strange man attempted to pet the adorable little rag mop of a dog, she would back away, crouch as if ready to spring, growl, and yap furiously. As I have mentioned, when Gus chased rabbits, he emitted a strange combination bark, bay, and whine.

Duffy had a typical small dog "yap, yap" with which he warned us of anyone approaching our front door. Two months after we obtained him, when he was nine months old, he was on our rear deck while I was in the adjacent family room, preparing to watch the San Francisco Giants play the Oakland A's in the World Series. Suddenly Duffy began his most vehement barking, his face pointed into the distance. Then I heard a sound that I took to be a low flying airplane. (We lived under the flight path of the nearby San Francisco International Airport.) I noticed that the sound was more like that of a freight train than an airplane—an incongruity since there were no local railroad tracks. Abruptly Duffy and the invisible train ran through our family room. It was the Loma Prieta earthquake, 7 point plus, and deadly. As it rumbled through our house, it toppled three huge bookcases, its shaking action deftly and gently depositing the books on the floor in perfect shelved order. It next struck the decorative copper pots and cooking utensils hung over the butcher block in our kitchen, causing them to bang into one another in a chilling cacophony. Then as suddenly as it came, it was gone, exiting through the attached garage. After that day, I always paid careful attention when Duffy barked.

Duffy was the only one of our dogs that ever watched television, growling and snapping at any animals that appeared—including cartoon dinosaurs and an occasional apelike human being—chasing them across the screen or jumping into the air in an attempt to bring them down, finally dashing in a tight circle around the TV set to make sure they were gone. A syndicated pet columnist insists that dogs cannot interpret the images on television. Duffy would have disagreed. Over the years, whenever I have seen strangers walking Westies, I stop and ask them if their dogs watch television. Over fifty percent claim that their dogs do!

During the last two or three years of his almost fourteen-year life, Duffy lost interest in TV and many of his other activities. Like Gus before him, he became a dog in retirement, content to nap near his people but unable to do much else.

Rizzi rarely barks except when she is on duty rounding up the horses. (This is the one time that cattle herding dogs are not supposed to bark!) Her bark is direct and businesslike. She barks in syllables; Nehi in complete sentences. At about 5:19 P.M. each day, she and Nehi remind me that it is dinnertime. Nehi "woo-woos" and scratches me while Rizzi uses my body as a springboard to jump up to the back of the sofa. After dinner, it is round-up time—Rizzi's principal job, which she handles with great élan. Whenever they can get away with it, both of the Aussie girls love to run the horses, dashing excitedly back and forth just outside their pasture fence, barking ferociously. No amount of dissuasion has broken them of this habit.

"Come!"

All of our animals know their own names but do they come when called? Sometimes.

Call any dog or cat by name, and Nehi will come immediately. Call Rizzi twice and she usually turns up no matter how far away she may have been, but not if she has something more interesting to do. Call Katie and, if you are lucky, she will look your way. She is a master of the game of selective hearing. Call Purr and she will take a message and get back to you when it suits her.

Rags is a sweetheart and a mooch. Just approach within two hundred yards of him and he will saunter over to see if you have any treats for him. Stormy is fairly good about responding when called but always resistant enough to remind you that she is the queen of the pasture.

They were up to something all right, but if they thought
Tassy was going to respond they had better guess again!

In Memoriam

This section is in tribute to the pets who have gone before, whom we miss terribly, and who live on in precious memories—Cuddles dancing, Gus chasing an elusive rabbit, Duffy attacking the TV, and Tassy magically appearing in our path.

Shayla and Friends Attend a Funeral

by Rev. Ralph C. Roth
August 7, 2002

[Ralph is my oldest and dearest friend. Although we are different in many ways, there is an underlying mysticism that unites us. It is hard to put in words, but it is undeniable. And there is the brotherly love between us that few men are lucky enough to share.

And, of course, there is our love for our animals.

Ralph wrote to me recently of a particularly moving animal experience. His account follows.]

It's never felt quite like home either to my wife Jean or me when we didn't have a dog around the house. Whenever nature required us to part with one of our faithful little ones, I insisted on preparing a grave, sometimes assisted by one of our three sons. Then everyone close enough to home at the time gathered round for the burial—always an event charged with emotion as we shared our grief and expressed appreciation, thanks, and fond memories. Only once would I be all alone in this experience—or so I thought.

In late February of 1989, Brandy, our female Beagle, who had loved and served us from puppyhood for thirteen years, fell gravely ill. Our vet recommended euthanasia then and there at the office. I called home to ask Jean's consensus and, tearfully expressing our love and appreciation, I held little Brandy in my arms till she exhaled her last breath.

The doctor offered to dispose of her body. "No," I said. "We always do a burial." "The ground is frozen solid," he replied, "but you could keep the body for a while in cold storage."

A plan took shape in my mind. I carried Brandy's corpse, carefully wrapped in heavy plastic bags, and on reaching home, powered up a spare refrigerator/freezer in our garage. In a few weeks the ground would thaw.

That night a possibility occurred to me. In February of the previous year our youngest, Jim, and his bride, Mandy, had purchased "Spring Hollow Farm," an eight-acre property with a restored farmhouse, large barn, horse stables, and nicely fenced pastures. It had appealed to them, especially as Mandy had since childhood always owned a horse. At the time of Brandy's death, the farm supported Shayla, Mandy's seventeen-year-old Arabian mare; Dutch, an elderly, retired national champion barrel racer; and five other horses for whom Mandy and Jim were providing board.

A phone call confirmed my guess that at the farm—some eighty miles south of where we lived—the ground had already thawed. "It certainly has," said Jim. "You can dig a grave just outside the lower fence of the pasture behind the barn." The next Monday—my day off from my duties as the rector of Trinity Episcopal Church in Mount Pocono—I would do so. I'd be alone this time since Jean would be at work, as would Jim and Mandy. Our other sons, Dave and Bill, were out of state, pursuing graduate studies.

At Spring Hollow Farm, Shayla had clearly established her dominance over the other horses. She was the unchallenged leader of the herd. Whenever Jean and I visited the farm, she would readily come close to Jean, Mandy, and any other woman present but would not allow Jim or me or any other male person to touch her.

Responding to my initial surprise, Mandy had explained her belief that some male must once have abused Shayla. The mare would simply have nothing to do with me. Only the male farrier—by some "gift of magic" could touch and control her. Needless to mention, I proved bereft of this special gift!

As I made my way to the farm with Brandy's body, it was a warm, clear day. Taking pick and shovel from the barn, I chose a site where Jim had suggested and dug a grave. Next I returned to my car for Brandy. As I fitted the key into the trunk lock, glancing across the pastures, I spied Shayla, Dutch, and the other five horses. They enjoyed free run of three interconnected pasture areas and just then were all together, grazing at the back of the far pasture, about 120 yards from where I was digging. A small copse of woods and thicket lay between their pasture and the burial site, hiding my activities.

With tears streaming down my cheeks, I bore my now unwrapped burden slowly toward the grave, climbed through the rail fence, and heaving great sobs, lowered Brandy's lifeless body gently into the earth. On my knees, clasping my hands, I scooped in the loose soil with my arms.

Suddenly I stopped as I sensed the unmistakable feeling on the back of my neck that someone was gazing at me close up. Still on my knees, I turned about, scarcely believing what I saw. Just eight feet away, there stood all of the horses, their heads close together, their necks resting on the top fence rail. Three horses stood on each side of Shayla, like great spokes on half a giant wagon wheel!

I struggled to my feet and slowly approached them, sobbing all the while. I threw my arms around the neck of Shayla—Shayla who had never permitted me to touch her or even feed her a carrot from my hand. I caressed her head and whispered appreciation. Then, in turn, I hugged and thanked Dutch and the others. All seven remained there, gazing at me, as I returned to my task and placed a large stone atop the mounded grave.

As I stood, I turned to see Shayla stepping back and slowly turning away. Her six companions followed, making their way behind her back whence they had come, in what seemed to me to be a solemn procession.

There I knew I had been in sacred space, caught up into sacred time. Shayla and her friends had been the channels of that marvelous grace.

Mandy wasn't the least surprised when that evening I told my tale. Through the years of owning and training horses she'd observed that they could be keenly aware of and tuned into human emotions—even from a distance—and are capable of heartfelt, enduring empathy.

Until Shayla's death two years ago, whenever Jean and I visited the farm, the mare would sense my presence and come to me for a little whisper and a fond embrace.

Years after Brandy's beautifully attended funeral, I came upon a counsel of Meister Eckhart, which, due to Shayla and her friends, I shall ever treasure in my heart:

> Apprehend God in all things for God is in all things.
> Every creature is full of God and is a book about God.
> Every creature is a word of God.
>
> If I spent enough time with the smallest creature—even a caterpillar—I would never have to write a sermon, so full of God is every creature.

After Reading About Shayla

My wife Connie also witnessed that special gift animals seem to possess when they experience the death of one of their own.

When her terminally ill cat disappeared, she searched the house and grounds for several days before she discovered Tassie taking her eternal nap under the hedge off the back deck.

She rounded up the dogs and put them in the house before she went to the shed for a shovel. She struggled to dig a hole—the ground was hard and full of roots.

Her heart ached as she wrapped Tassie in a cloth and moved her. She had been such a sweet little cat. She recalled how thin she was when she came to us, just bones it seemed—and how dull and brittle her black coat was. True, she had been though a lot—a serious infection, neglect. And even shot at. But with love and affection directed at her, good nutrition and regular meals, she had flourished. Even all the dogs welcomed her to share their space.

"I hope you don't mind, but Lowell ate
some of your cat food.
He thought it was tuna casserole!"

Tassie was Connie's companion in the garden as she watered or pruned the roses. The cat would rub up against her leg for a little attention or follow from place to place, her long black tail hovering straight above her like an antenna. It was as if she had built-in radar in that tail. Wherever Connie was headed, the garden or the barn, she seemed to just appear there ahead of her. How did she do that?

After Connie gathered some river rocks and arranged them over the mound of dirt, she selected one of her garden markers to memorialize Tassie—a stone engraved, "Joy." Tassie had been a joy to us.

With the last stone in place Connie went to the house to tell me and to take me to the spot she had selected under the cypress tree.

As we walked to the far corner of the yard, the three dogs—Katie the Scottie, Duffy the Westie, and Nehi the Queensland—bounced around at our feet. I walked ahead, and then stood near the small mound of rocks waiting for the others to catch up. As they made a sharp turn and came into view, I noticed Nehi stiffen her front legs. She emitted a low growl. The hair on her neck and all along her back stood up about four inches. She threw her head back and howled a desperate wail. She then approached, sniffed around, and withdrew.

I don't know what happened there in that moment but Nehi was definitely affected.

It still haunts us when we think back on it.

Rainbow Bridge

Just this side of heaven is a place called Rainbow Bridge. When an animal dies that has been especially close to someone here, that pet goes to Rainbow Bridge. There are meadows and hills for all our special friends so they can run and play together. There is plenty of food, water, and sunshine, and our friends are warm and comfortable.

All the animals who have been ill and old are restored to health and vigor; those who were hurt or maimed are made whole and strong again, just as we remember them in our dreams of days and times gone by. The animals are happy and content, except for one small thing: they each miss someone very special to them, who had to be left behind.

They all run and play together, but the day comes when one suddenly stops and looks into the distance. His bright eyes are intent; his eager body quivers. Suddenly, he begins to run from the group, flying over the green grass, his legs carrying him faster and faster.

You have been spotted, and when you and your special friend finally meet, you cling together in joyous reunion, never to be parted again. The happy kisses rain upon your face; your hands again caress the beloved head, and you look once more into the trusting eyes of your pet, so long gone from your life but never absent from your heart.

Then you cross Rainbow Bridge together . . . .

—Author unknown

The Grief of Pet Loss

Because individuals come to view their pets as members of the family, grieving people experience both physical and emotional traumas as they try to adapt to the upheaval in their lives brought about by their pet loss. The death of a pet means the loss of a nonjudgmental love source, and thus, when compared with human loss, in many ways is less ambivalent. Pet loss can be profound because there is no longer anything for the pet owner to nurture and care for, the owner loses contact with the world of nature, social contacts may be disrupted, and all the positive benefits of pet ownership cease. These feelings of loss can be particularly intense for the elderly, single people, and childless couples.

Pet illness and loss is similar to that experienced at the loss of a human companion. Pet owners go through similar stages of grief. Initially there is agitation, denial, and isolation. Anger may accompany denial or may come later.

The next stage is overt grief and fear. This may impede the owner's letting go of the pet in a timely manner, and allowing it to be put out of its misery through euthanasia. The pet owner may also project his own fears about death onto his animal. It is helpful to understand that people's greatest anxiety about death is the fear of dying, not death itself, and that animals do not have an awareness of death.

Resolution is the final stage in the process. The owner eventually comes to accept the inevitability of the pet's death and can then move on to help his pet.

The loss of a loved pet may not be as traumatic as that of a family member, but it also can be great enough to have some adverse health consequences. The depth and intensity of the mourning process depends on many factors. Given time, healing will occur for the bereaved owner. The owner should give herself permission to grieve and accept the feelings that come with grief.

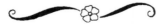

—Jessica Barrett

"The congregation wants you to know that everyone is too busy to visit, but they decided to pray for your recovery—by a vote of 43 to 39!"

With Us Always

Before I retired I thought I was an important person. After I retired I felt like a nobody. How could I be so wrong twice?

—Rev. Bob Kemper, retired minister

Cottonwood, California, 2003. I left the parish ministry ten years ago. No. I was not *defrocked*; just *unsuited*—not the right person for a congregation of well-educated, prosperous, demanding senior citizens. I just could not make them happy, I was told, as if I were solely responsible for their happiness. I did the best I could. I preached well-received sermons—a hundred of them were published in various homiletic journals and in my book, *Pastor's Complete Handbook of Model Sermons.* I visited the sick, comforted the bereaved, served on my denomination's conference board of directors, and chaired the Spiritual Development Network of the United Church of Christ. Nevertheless, I did not make enough of my congregants happy. And when, in the midst of my ministry, I was hospitalized for cancer surgery, not one officer of the church visited me!

My four years (1989-93) with the church provided me with a stable income for the only time since 1979. For most of my adult life, including the ten years since I resigned as pastor, I have supported myself through a variety of entrepreneurial undertakings—writing, counseling, consulting, and part-time teaching.

Even more difficult than staying afloat financially has been the need to structure my time and ration my waning energies. I was fifty-four when I left the parish ministry, recovering from two unrelated cancers, two major surgeries, chemotherapy, depression, and diabetes. Back then I was told that I had a life expectancy of two years!

Today, I am sixty-four. I fight chronic exhaustion and must nap for an hour or two after lunch each day. Glaucoma and cataracts limit my vision. My teeth are deserting me like faithless lovers. My libido, once in overdrive, has settled into an early retirement.

". . . and we hold you personally responsible for the extremely uncomfortable temperature in this church!"

When I have something significant to do, I have the get-up-and-go to do it. When I do not have anything significant to do, I would just as well watch the History Channel or CNN. If it were not for the animals, I might not get up some mornings. By 6 A.M., Rizzi is climbing over my turned back, scratching my arms, and licking my face and neck. I lead her to the kitchen, let her and her sister dogs out into the backyard, let Purr in, start the morning coffee, feed Purr, feed the dogs, unload the dishwasher, fill clean cups with coffee and take them to Connie, who is still in bed.

The three dogs follow me to the bedroom. The Aussie girls jump into the bed, struggle to remove the covers that Connie has by now thrown over her head, play with one another as I lift short-legged Katie into the bed so that she can drape herself over Connie's reclining body. After a few minutes of frantic activity featuring much face-licking, nuzzling, and pawing of both of their humans, the dogs settle down as if napping while Connie and I drink our first cup of coffee of the day and watch *Good Morning, America*. After a half an hour, Nehi decides it is time for us to get up and issues her emphatic cry of "woo-woo!" We pull on our morning barn clothes and our manure-resistant footgear, chop some carrots and slice an apple, and head for the stable. Rizzi leaps the fence ahead of us and races to the barn to bark at the paddock-confined horses before we call her off and secure her with an extra long leash to our round pen.

Since Stormy's paddock is closest to us, we interact with her first while Rags drifts about in his enclosure. Stormy's responses to us are as varied as her moods. One morning, she will reach her massive neck and head over the gate and nuzzle my hand with a soft, lips-only kiss. Sometimes she will lightly nibble at my hand or clothes. Other mornings, she will turn away toward the gate to the pasture and pay us no heed. Now and then, just as we approach, she will lift her tail, move it to one side, and pee a gallon or two. (My horse-loving friends say that this is a "good thing.")

I place two flakes of grass hay/alfalfa (about ten pounds) in a large plastic bucket and take them into the pasture with Stormy walking beside me, step by step. She takes a few trial bites as I dump one flake on the ground for her and another flake fifen or twenty feet away for Rags, who is nervously trying to pick the clasp to the chain that holds him in his paddock. Connie or I release him and he high steps his way, half cantering, half bucking, to his flake. Soon Stormy will come and claim his food, and he will meekly wander over to where she had been eating. They may repeat this dance several times.

While Connie rakes the manure in their paddocks and the manure and wet shavings in their stalls into neat piles, I prepare the meal they will eat when they are put up for the evening. First, I take an additional flake to each stall and place it in a wall-hung manger. Then I return to the tack and hay room, and in two green bowls about the diameter of pie tins but twice as deep, I mix a cup of grain, a daily dewormer, a joint rejuvenator, and whatever other supplements they may require plus the chopped carrots and apple segments.

I give Stormy's bowl to Connie and head to Rags' paddock, where he awaits me on the other side of the pipe fence. If Connie is slow in getting into position with Stormy, the big mare approaches me and Rags shows his respect and wanders off once again. But I do not feed her and wait for Connie to lure her away so that Rags may return. They usually snort impatiently until they receive their morning treats. Rags trained me to add this daily ritual to their morning feedings. He would see me carrying that green bowl toward his manger and complain with soulful whinnies and snorts and hang his head over the fence until I saved some of its contents to offer to him. I don't think Stormy caught on for two years!

Next we rake up the stalls and paddocks, load up the wheelbarrow, and head out to the back of the pasture to dump the contents in our

RON

Of course Connie never smoked them,
but rolling them just looked so western!

ever-growing manure heap. Horses have not been told about the law of conservation of matter. For every ton they eat, they produce two tons of waste! While we are raking and shoveling, I cannot help but think of that joke my dad, "the thief of bad gags," liked to tell me when I was a college student—you know, what "B.S." and "M.S." stand for and that "Ph.D." means "piled higher and deeper"! Little did he know what his son, a Princeton Ph.D., would be doing in his sixties!

Stormy is content to work away at her food, while Rags tends to walk over to us, hoping that we will have some more treats for him or a least some strokes and pats. Stormy resents being disturbed while she is eating and she flattens her ears straight back so that we will know. Then we fit their fly masks over their heads, secure the various gates, and unfasten Rizzi. Sometimes Connie lingers behind to sweep up the loose hay in the tack room.

It is now Nehi's Jolly Ball time. I throw; she retrieves; Rizzi runs with her but seldom touches the ball; and Katie surveys the action from a discreet distance as she devotedly waits at the gate for Connie's return from the barn. Then Rizzi and I walk through the garage and out to the street, where our morning paper waits in its separate container next to the mailbox. I keep Rizzi on a lead and reinforce her training—sit, heel, sit stay, down—as we stroll the gravel driveway to and from the street.

By now it is close to nine o'clock and our day has begun. After breakfast, I download my e-mail and get to work on my writing projects or preparing for classes. By mid-afternoon, the dogs surround me as I nap or continue to write. Right now, Rizzi is asleep under my desk, Nehi snoozes to my left, and Katie lies a few feet away in the hallway. Their presence is a comfort and a reassurance. I look out the window and watch the horses, grazing contentedly in the sunlight. No matter what I may achieve in life, nothing gives me more sense of accomplishment and fulfillment than my dogs, cats, and horses.

For my generation, modern life has scattered family members to the four winds. As much as I want to nurture and be nurtured by my family, there are precious few of them at hand. My daughter lives in Los Angeles; my son in New Jersey. His son lives with his mother in a suburb of Kansas City. My wife's sons and her three grandchildren live hours away. I thank God that I have the animals to look after, to be my companions, to need me, and to be needed by me. Our four children

RON

"It's hard to believe that a mutual interest in shoveling horse manure has kept you two together all these years!"

are adults. They live at a distance—geographically and in other ways. We see them, converse with them, hug them and are hugged by them all too infrequently. When we manage to get together for those special occasions, we have our good times, sharing stories to fill in the gaps in our knowledge of one another's day-to-day triumphs and frustrations.

But this is not too often. Of course, Connie and I are here for them and their own four children—Jonathan, Justin, Jacob, and Jessica—when they need us and when they are available. But the animals are always with us: loving, demanding, giving, and taking, always . . . .

"Connie? Aggie? . . . Could it be Jessie? . . .
Don't tell me . . . !"

Up to Date

Cottonwood, California, April 2004. Several months have passed since I wrote the preceding chapters. Connie, Katie, Nehi, Rizzi, Purr, Stormy, and Rags are still healthy and happy on Lone Pine Ranch, our home in the country.

Katie has lived long past the life expectancy for her breed and is amazingly youthful—much more so than Cuddles, Gus, and Duffy were in old age. Of course, she leads a sedate and undemanding existence.

Nehi decided that it was unfair for us to allow Rizzi to sleep with us and proved that she too could escape from confinement. So she joined Rizzi, snuggling up with us in our bed at night. That left the Katie deprived and bereft, so I invited her to our bedroom.

Soon the dogs divided the territory among themselves: Nehi acquiring the space at our feet, Rizzi curling up in the armchair next to my side of the bed, and Katie spurning a large, soft mat, squeezing herself instead into a tiny foam bed designed for one cat!

Nehi and Rizzi have worked out a signal system. In the evening, Rizzi waits just outside the pasture for my approach so that she can discharge her duties by rounding up the horses. As I open the back door to the house and step out, Nehi signals my imminent arrival with a distinctive "woof, woo!" Then Rizzi springs into action and gathers her herd. This done, she awaits a "good job, Rizzi" response from me and heads to the house, her head high, her chest swollen with pride.

The Aussie girls' latest game is tag team fetch. Until recently, when I threw the Jolly Ball, Nehi would leap into action and retrieve it by its handle and return it to me while Rizzi ran a parallel course near her, urging her on but never touching the ball. In the past few weeks, Nehi has taken to grasping the ball by its body and offering the handle to Rizzi so that they can carry it back to me in tandem. At first I thought that this pattern was a coincidence, but it has now proved to be standard behavior.

The New Kids

From time to time, Connie would express how deeply she felt the loss of her cat. Finding another cat seemed a logical solution, but logic is one thing and emotions are another.

I broached the subject on several occasions but she expressed reservations. Before long, these were reduced to a list of negatives: no kittens, no male cats, no orange cats, and no longhaired cats. Logic was at work once more!

Mary, a local cat rescuer, advertised in the daily newspaper, "Barn cats and other cats for adoption." Our area is rich in caring volunteers who offer sanctuary, foster homes, placement, and, when necessary, hospice services for companion animals, wildlife, birds, stray domestic farm animals, and even six-foot-tall emus that have been released in the wild when they have proved unprofitable investments.

We phoned Mary and made arrangements to visit her home, where sixty-five cats, many of them feral felines that Mary trapped in the middle of many a night, were in foster residence. Mary, a registered nurse, not only feeds and houses her cats, but administers medications, takes them to local veterinarians for treatment, and sees to it that they are spayed or neutered. Mary's cats are the smallest percentage of the unwanted, abandoned, and feral felines in our county—the product of uncaring, careless, and irresponsible pet owners.

Connie looked the animals over and was attracted to a longhaired, female tortoiseshell cat slightly larger than Purr. Among the scores of cats, this "tortie" was the only one that approached Connie and rubbed against Connie's leg. The cat has a distinctive marking, an inverted "Y" or wishbone on her forehead, and large, hypnotic amber eyes. A Redding family had moved from their apartment and simply left the pet to fend for herself.

We took the cat home and set up a new "Kitty City" for her in our guest bedroom. She retreated behind a sofa and greeted all efforts to extract her, pet her, or even touch her with claws and fangs. Daily, I tended my wounds and swore that I was going to return her to Mary.

But before I could do this, Mary phoned and told Connie about feral kittens, malnourished brothers that she had trapped behind a local business. One looked like a ring-tailed, blue-eyed Siamese. The other was a "tuxedo cat" similar to Connie's beloved Tassie.

When we brought the kittens home, they needed frequent feedings of goat milk, rice cereal, and baby food chicken. Nilla (so called because he is the color of a Vanilla Wafer) would cuddle up with Ginger. So now we have four cats: the formidable Ginger; the two small boys, Smudge and Nilla; and, of course, Purr. Ginger has long since decided to keep us and comes to me constantly to be petted, to run her tail through my fingers, or to sit in my lap. (She is doing these things even as I type!) Then without warning, she will yelp, slap at my hand, and run off.

Smudge, the tuxedo cat, named for a small black spot beside his nose on his mostly white face, is loving, playful, and appreciative. He starts purring the moment Connie or I make eye contact with him!

Nilla is shy, a proverbial scaredy-cat. Get within two feet of him and he will scamper away. When he is in the house, he has a habit of staying within two feet of us, wherever we may be, but never allowing us to come in contact with him. However, he has two daily moments of vulnerability: when he is eating and when he comes to rest on the sofa in the evening when I am watching television. At these times, I can move stealthily to him and pet him, which he obviously loves. Sometimes in the evenings, I even lift him into my lap and he remains there as I stroke his soft body. He naps and purrs softly. At such times, I feel as though I have accomplished something audaciously grand! Then suddenly he remembers who he is and where he is, becomes hyper-alert, and runs away.

Frequently one of the larger cats finds her way to our bed at night before we do, Ginger on my pillow until I move her or Purr firmly planted between where we will slumber. There one of the cats sleeps with people and dogs all around her. (When I shut down the computer and went to bed, Purr was waiting!)
So now our family includes:

> Smudge the Adorable
> Nilla the Timid
> Ginger the Fearsome

The Aussie girls and the kittens seem genuinely fond of one another and often exchange nuzzles and sniffs. Purr ignores the new animals but there has been one definite change in her behavior. We had planned on recruiting ferocious Ginger for the task of being our barn cat. Purr obviously overheard the discussions and took up the assignment on her own! She assiduously patrols the tack room, where the grain and hay are stored, jumping from bale to bale, sniffing every nook and cranny, filling her long, luxurious fur with barn debris. Her accomplishments as a mouser remain a mystery. Thus far, she has neither brought us a mouse nor left evidence of a mousicide. But the mice are no longer in evidence as they were before she began her guard duty. (Note: The morning after writing this, I found two freshly slain mice in Stormy's stall! Purr was the only cat that spent the night out of doors—the night after she slept between Connie and me. Be careful what you think. Your pets are listening!)

Like Purr, Ginger primarily associates with us humans and avoids contact with the other animals. If Purr or one of the kittens gets in her face, Ginger will hiss or even emit the growling roar of a jungle feline. Other times, she will allow timid Nilla to snuggle with her.

Stormy has a new hobby. She hangs over the back pasture fence, entranced by a neighbor's mama llama and her recently born baby.

Rags continues to take good care of me, making sure that I never do anything foolhardy like asking him to gallop or jump fences. He recognizes and observes my limitations. As a result, I have suffered no additional falls.

And Then There Were Five!

Sherry, Connie's cousin, lives three miles from us in Cottonwood. She works at the local high school where she has undertaken the rescue of many cats that have been abandoned on the campus. One of these was a beautiful, smallish Siamese, whose tawny fur is splashed with muted streaks of black. The cat had been living in a junked car belonging to the high school auto repair class.

Sherry called on Mary for assistance. They captured the animal and took her to Mary's feline sanctuary for proper attention. As it turned out, hunger and loneliness were not the cat's only problems. She required immediate veterinary attention for distemper and a hernia. After treatment, corrective surgery, and spaying, the cat was named Lily and, thanks to her affectionate, outgoing, and amiable nature, soon became Mary's favorite.

With her cousin, Connie visited Mary and came home with such glowing accounts of the cat that I phoned Mary while Connie was at work and asked if Mary wanted to place Lily for adoption. She was reluctant but promised to consider it.

Connie was uncomfortable with the thought of taking Mary's personal pet but Mary soon came to the conclusion that with more than eighty cats to look after, it would be best for Lily if she found a permanent home. So last Sunday Mary arrived at our home with Lily in a pet carrier.

Lily is now a happy member of our family. None of our companion animals has ever contentedly fit in so readily. We expected her to conceal herself in some hidey-hole until she ascertained the situation in general and the temperament of our dogs and cats in particular. But Lily is an extrovert, exploring every inch of our home, approaching Connie and me to be stroked or played with, and rubbing noses with both dogs and cats. The Aussie girls and the little boys have accepted her while the two larger cats, Purr and Ginger, maintain their distance. Katie, our elderly Scottie, just shakes her graying head in disbelief!

Are five cats too many? If we had not gotten to know animal champions such as Mary, who lovingly and heroically rescues homeless cats, and Rita Reynolds, who wrote the foreword to this book and who currently cares for nineteen cats, eight dogs, and assorted other animals, we might have thought so. But there are just so many destitute animals. Our county shelter is overflowing with unwanted dogs and cats, more than ten thousand of which are euthanized there yearly. The care and feeding of a few companions is a small contribution to make to an overwhelming problem.

Welcome, Lily the Affable. Live Long and Prosper!

Garrison Keillor always ends his most famous monologues with the words: "And that's the news from Lake Woebegone, where the women are strong, the men are good-looking, and all the children are above average." And I end mine by saying, "Goodbye from Lone Pine Ranch in Cottonwood, California, where the horses graze contentedly, the birds croon, the frogs and toads serenade, the cats are in their cradles, and Lowell and Connie sleep their three-dog nights."

Afterword:
The Human/Companion Animal Bond

The medical community today acknowledges the importance of our connection to the world of companion animals. In their physical role, pets contribute increased exercise, sensory stimulation, decreased blood pressure, the comfort of touch, and a diversion from pain. Animals provide emotional benefits as they shower us with unconditional love and attention, allow spontaneous expression of emotion, reduce our loneliness, decrease our anxiety, and provide us with increased relaxation and fun. Our pets provide social benefits as well, such as providing security; relieving the boredom, monotony and isolation of life; and allowing us the opportunity to communicate with an animal and to others about our animal.

Living with a pet is like living with an instant relaxation therapist. Anyone who has ever sat stroking a dog's ears or scratching a cat's head while it purrs contentedly understands how stress-relieving a pet can be. Although having a pet is not a cure, it does go a long way toward helping patients recover from mental and physical illness.

Pets increase the survival rate of heart attack victims. Owning a pet can reduce blood pressure as efficiently as a low salt diet or cutting down on alcohol.

Our animals improve morale and give us a feeling of support during periods of illness. Pets distract us from worry, make us feel more secure, stimulate physical activity, make us laugh, and help us feel needed.

Pets help all of us—young and old—hold onto the world of reality, of care, of human toil and sacrifice, and of intense emotional relationships. Our self-concept as worthwhile individuals is restored and even enhanced when we find that the pet we have been caring for loves us in return. Pets help the elderly cope with the loss of a loved one or a change in their circumstances. Pet owners are too connected to the world of pets and activities through their pets to feel the same isolation and desperation that the aging non-pet owner might feel. Pet owners are never at a loss for humor and laughter— and laughter has been shown to be therapeutic. It can fight off illness and even promotes healing.

To pet lovers, companion animals are true miracle workers.

—Jessica Barrett

Also by Lowell D. Streiker

Author:

Pet Tales, Wasteland Press, 2003.

The Little Book of Laughter, Thomas Nelson Publishers, 2001.

Nelson's Amazing Bible Trivia, Thomas Nelson Publishers, 2001.

Nelson's Big Book of Laughter from A to Z, Thomas Nelson Publishers, 2000.

A Treasury of Humor, Hendrickson Publishers, 2000.

Smith's Friends: An American Religion Critic Meets a Free-Church Movement, Praeger, 1999.

An Encyclopedia of Humor, Hendrickson Publishers, 1998.

Laughter in the House of God, Edgewater Press, 1995, also e-book.

Pastor's Complete Handbook of Model Sermons, Prentice Hall, 1992.

New Age Comes to Main Street, Abingdon Press, 1990.

Fathering—Old Game, New Rules, Abingdon Press, 1989.

Family, Friends, and Strangers: Every Christian's Guide to Counseling, Abingdon Press, 1988.

The Gospel Time Bomb: Ultrafundamentalism and the Future of America, Prometheus Press, 1985.

Mind-Bending: Brainwashing, Cults, and Deprogramming in the '80s, Doubleday, 1984.

Cults, Abingdon Press, 1983.

The Cults Are Coming! Abingdon Press, 1978.

The Jesus Trip, Abingdon Press, 1971.

The Gospel of Irreligious Religion, Sheed and Ward, 1969.

The Promise of Buber, Lippincott, 1969.

Co-author:

Religion and the New Majority: Billy Graham, Middle America and the Politics of the '70s, Association Press, 1972.

Modern Theologians: Christians and Jews, Notre Dame, 1967.

Editor:

Who Am I? Second Thoughts on Man, His Loves, His Gods, Sheed and Ward, 1970.

Rev. Lowell's Treasury of Humor, 8 volumes, electronic books on CD ROM :
He Who Laughs, Lasts
Signs of the Times
Laughter in the House of God
Legal Beagles and Courthouse Hounds
Star Spangled Banter
Quotable Quotes
Family Follies
Who Am I?

Contributor:
Friendship, St. Mary's Press, 2004.
The Need for a Second Look at Jonestown: Remembering Its People, Edwin Mellen Press, 1989.
Welcome at God's Table: 1992-1993 Worship Program Book, UCC, 1992.
GRAND-Stories: 101 Bridges of love joining grandparents and grandkids, Friendly Oaks Publications, 2000.
Religion for a New Generation, Macmillan, 1973.

Audiotape:
Every Christian's Guide to Counseling, 1989.

Other Alpine Titles
You Might Enjoy:

Cleo and Cindy: What Two Dogs Taught Me About Unconditional Friendship, Jack Dempsey, Foreword by George Page.
ISBN 1-57779-070-7

Experiences Along the Way: What I've Learned About Horses, Joe Andrews.
ISBN 1-57779-044-8

Miracle Dog: How Quentin Survived the Gas Chamber to Speak for Animals on Death Row, Randy Grim, Foreword by Dr. Jane Goodall.
ISBN 1-57779-071-5

**For a complete catalog of Alpine titles,
Call 1-800-777-7257
fax 1-970-667-9157
email alpinecsr@aol.com
or visit our website: www.alpinepub.com**